THE STOIC ART OF RECOVERY

THE STOIC ART OF RECOVERY

The Roman Stoics as Spiritual Guides to Twelve-Step Living

MICHAEL MASCIO

BLOOMSBURY ACADEMIC
NEW YORK • LONDON • OXFORD • NEW DELHI • SYDNEY

BLOOMSBURY ACADEMIC
Bloomsbury Publishing Inc, 1359 Broadway, New York, NY 10018, USA
Bloomsbury Publishing Plc, 50 Bedford Square, London, WC1B 3DP, UK
Bloomsbury Publishing Ireland, 29 Earlsfort Terrace, Dublin 2, D02 AY28, Ireland

First published in the United States of America 2026

Cover design: Jen Huppert Design
Cover image © Raica Tarr, 2024

A catalog record for this book is available from the Library of Congress.

ISBN: HB: 979-8-8818-0830-3
ePDF: 979-8-7651-5194-5
eBook: 979-8-8818-0831-0

Typeset by Integra Software Services Pvt. Ltd.
Printed and bound in the United States of America

For product safety-related questions, contact productsafety@bloomsbury.com.

To find out more about our authors and books visit www.bloomsbury.com and sign up for our newsletters.

CONTENTS

FOREWORD

Some books arrive like a steady hand on the tiller. *The Stoic Art of Recovery* is one of them. Calm, clear, and oriented toward what actually helps, it offers a simple promise that is kept on every page: the wisdom of the Roman Stoics can be lived, not merely admired, and it can serve people in Twelve-Step recovery today. Michael Mascio, who is an accomplished Classicist and a sober member of Alcoholics Anonymous, translates the Stoics' philosophy into everyday practice without jargon or gatekeeping. He shows how *logos* (reason), *phusis* (nature), and what AA sometimes calls "Good Orderly Direction"—seeking guidance from others who have walked the path—can point to a power that is real, dependable, and open to atheist, agnostic, and believer alike. Thus, readers who cannot muster up the religious faith to accept the motto, *credo quia absurdum* (I believe *because* it is absurd) will find in this volume a more down-to-earth path to spiritual health. Mascio's aim is not to argue anyone out of their tradition, but to widen the path so that more can walk it.

One finds three marvelous gifts in this volume. **First, it reframes recovery as a craft.** Drawing on Epictetus' favorite metaphor of the athlete in training, it recasts sobriety as *askesis*: deliberate, daily practice. The image is nonjudgmental and motivating at once. Instead of "fix yourself," we are told to *train steadily, build the muscles you will need before the fight begins.* "Ninety in ninety," morning meditation, the Tenth-Step inventory, and phone calls to a sponsor become the repetitions that lead to strength. Relapse is not the end of the story. It is the call to reenter the contest. Epictetus' **dichotomy of control** aligns seamlessly with the "Serenity Prayer." Focus on what is up to you (attention, choices, effort), relinquish what is not (outcomes, others' reactions, the sometimes harsh weather of life), and that pairing alone can carry a person through rough waters.

Second, Mascio puts tools in your hand. The book's *armamentarium* is a toolbox, not a museum case, and it works. *Objective representation* (seeing a fact as a fact before adding a judgment) pairs with *suspension of assent* (pausing before we say "this is awful" or "I can't bear it"). Practiced together, they look remarkably like the most effective elements of Cognitive Behavioral Therapy, and for good reason. The book explains that lineage without ever losing its practical focus. You will also meet *praemeditatio malorum* (rehearsing difficulties in advance) and the Stoic *reserve clause* ("I will do X *if fate permits*"). AA members will recognize the echoes of "just for today," "easy does it," and the wise sponsorship that says, *do the footwork, but let go of the results.* Taken together, these techniques cut the wire between that first involuntary surge of feeling and the destructive passion that follows if we fuse event and judgment into one.

Third, serenity is restored to its rightful place. Seneca's chosen word *tranquillitas* means more than a stiff upper lip and a calm face. It evokes a calm inner sea. Using this living metaphor, the book draws a picture most of us long for, *in media tempestate tranquillitas* (serenity in the midst of a storm). That is the nature of emotional sobriety. Not the becalmed life of avoidance, but the skilled sailor's poise with sheets trimmed, attention wakeful, course adjusted as rough conditions keep changing. This vision is not airy or dependent on faith; it is earned through the work of Chapters 1 and 2 and sustained by the rhythms of Chapter 5, which is focused on the importance of time. Own the present day as the only harbor that is ours. Seneca's bracing counsel *to reclaim yourself for yourself and gather and guard your time* lands in recovery with special force. One day well-lived is enough. It is also the only thing any of us ever receive.

The overall plan of the book is both reflective and humane. Each of the three major Stoics becomes a guide for a facet of sober living. **Epictetus** is the guide for habits, self-formation, and the athlete's mind. Progress, not perfection, is rendered philosophically sturdy. **Seneca** is enlisted for serenity, metaphor, and the gentle discipline that turns seasickness into balance. Finally, **Marcus Aurelius** teaches reliance on the nonsectarian power of nature that we approach not through anxious prayer, but by learning new ways of paying attention to it.

Along the way, Mascio illuminates the affinities between Stoicism and modern therapy, between Twelve-Step suggestions and ancient insights, and, unexpectedly and fruitfully, between Stoicism and the *Tao Te Ching.* These are not just clever scholarly parallels for their own sake or displays of the author's erudition. They are invitations to experiment. Read a few lines of Marcus or Laozi, step outside, breathe the air, and notice that acceptance sometimes sounds like a breeze rustling the leaves.

Above all, the book is absolutely honest about difficulty. The odds of long-term sobriety can sound stark when stripped of anonymity and wishful thinking. Here, difficulty is not a verdict; it is a training weight. Epictetus asks for hard opponents because they make us strong. In the language of AA, we must learn the paradox of *accepting hardship as the pathway to our ease and peace.* Resentment is the number one offender and therefore must be carefully treated with the attention it deserves, and with the effective tools of objective description, reframing, gratitude, and making appropriate amends. In taking the reader through all of this, Mascio never shames or bullies. He coaches. For readers new to recovery, let Epictetus from the very outset teach you how to think about "ninety in ninety" as the beginning of a new *ethos.* For the true Stoic, this means not just new behavior, but a new way of being. Pair the "Serenity Prayer" with the Stoic dichotomy of control and always keep beside you as a small reminder these three questions: *What is up to me? What is not? What is the next right action?* Then see what changes. For battle-hardened veterans, Chapters 3 and 5 repay slow reading. Seneca's ship-of-soul image deepens the patience many years can teach, and his letter on time mirrors with an almost shocking specificity AA's daily design for living. If your practice has started to go a little stale, let these pages widen and reenergize it. Marcus' pages on nature, when read on a park bench or a porch, can redirect and refocus the attention of skeptic and believer alike.

Counselors, chaplains, and family members will find in this book a shared vocabulary. It reduces the friction and distraction that sometimes arise when people hear religious language they cannot accept or philosophical language they mistrust. Words like *askesis* (practice), *apatheia* (freedom from emotional turmoil), and *oikeiosis* (growing into what is naturally ours) are introduced with care and translated into daily actions of morning meditation, evening inventory, service, study, and fellowship. The glossary at the end is a gift of time-travel; the endnotes will reward anyone who wants to go deeper.

The transformation that this book proposes is admittedly not flashy. Rather, it is the durable kind. From reaction to response, from control to consent, from isolation to fellowship, from "success" and "failure" to honesty and effort. It is what AA calls "a daily reprieve" and what the Stoics call "a good flow of life." It is what a person looks like who can be cheerful and grave, and who can say, *"My life is turbulent at the moment, and I am handling it."*

A foreword really can only try to do two things if it is to be honest. It can situate a work and recommend it. Consider it situated. You hold a book in your hands that marries rigorous classical learning with the humility and humor of the sort of people who sit in rec centers and the basements of office buildings, and who tell the truth. Consider it recommended and with the greatest warmth and utmost confidence. Treat it as a morning companion, as a guide for sponsee conversations, a way to translate the "Serenity Prayer" into muscle memory. Keep it near your chair. Let its pages remind you that philosophy, at its best, is an art of living (*ars vitae*) not of merely existing. Be reminded that sobriety, at its best, is not grim abstinence but happy and joyous freedom. Let *The Stoic Art of Recovery* steady your hands, clear your sight, and return you to the present. That is where your will and deepest self *lives*, and where peace finds you. It is where the next right action is always possible.

Phillip Mitsis

Alexander S. Onassis Professor of Hellenic Culture and Civilization, Professor of Classics and Hellenic Studies, and affiliated Professor of Philosophy and Medieval and Renaissance Studies at New York University

THE TWELVE STEPS OF ALCOHOLICS ANONYMOUS

1. We admitted we were powerless over alcohol—that our lives had become unmanageable.
2. Came to believe that a Power greater than ourselves could restore us to sanity.
3. Made a decision to turn our will and our lives over to the care of God *as we understood Him*.
4. Made a searching and fearless moral inventory of ourselves.
5. Admitted to God, to ourselves, and to another human being the exact nature of our wrongs.
6. Were entirely ready to have God remove all these defects of character.
7. Humbly asked Him to remove our shortcomings.
8. Made a list of all persons we had harmed, and became willing to make amends to them all.
9. Made direct amends to such people wherever possible, except when to do so would injure them or others.
10. Continued to take personal inventory and when we were wrong promptly admitted it.
11. Sought through prayer and meditation to improve our conscious contact with God *as we understood Him*, praying only for knowledge of His will for us and the power to carry that out.
12. Having had a spiritual awakening as the result of these steps, we tried to carry this message to alcoholics and to practice these principles in all our affairs.

Introduction

The impetus for this book was my combined experience as a professional Classicist focused on teaching, researching, and writing on Classical philosophy and my personal experience as an alcoholic with over eleven years of continuous sobriety as a member of Alcoholics Anonymous.

After I had survived the initial detoxification phase and begun to put together continuous weeks of sobriety by attending AA meetings, reading recovery literature (both AA and non-AA), and getting to know certain members of AA who took me under their wing, I began to contemplate the nature of a spiritual path that could speak to me alongside the voices of AA.

I turned to the Stoics, with whom I had long been interested, for additional strength and guidance. During my early forays into morning meditations as recommended by the Eleventh Step,[1] I would read a passage from *Daily Reflections*, AA's most popular daily reader, and then one from the *Discourses* of Epictetus (*c.* 50–135 CE), a Roman Stoic lecturer who wrote in Greek. As I become more comfortable with sobriety and more interested in recovery, I varied my sources for both recovery and Stoic wisdom, branching out to incorporate meditation books from Hazelden Publishing as well as Buddhist and Taoist texts. I included the full panoply of Roman Stoics in addition to Epictetus, such as Musonius Rufus, Marcus Aurelius, Seneca, and others, mostly forgotten.

Over the next several years I began to live an AA life that was intellectually and spiritually informed by the Stoics. In doing so, I realized that a serious philosophical underpinning for the suggestions of AA and the recovery way of life could not only help many who are spiritual seekers, but especially those who have a difficult time separating the wisdom of Twelve-Step recovery from its Christian language and ethics. While AA as a community proudly embraces Buddhists, Taoists, and other spiritualists who are not religious and several volumes on Asian philosophy and recovery have appeared, I know of no work that offers a Stoic way of life as a philosophical adjutant to the spiritual awakening recovery requires. I set to work on this book intending it to be three things: a resource for the recovering person to find their own guidelines for such a life; a useful reference for those who work in the recovery field for what a philosophically informed recovery might look like; and an example of the application of a rigorous Stoicism to a set of very real-life problems. My belief is that it will also hold a good deal of interest to spiritual seekers more generally and to those who either dabble or work professionally in ancient philosophy.

The unique suitability of the way of life of the Roman Stoics Epictetus, Seneca, and Marcus Aurelius to the recovery journey of the addict and alcoholic in Twelve-Step recovery is not as surprising as it might seem at first. One might be tempted to wonder what the particular Roman version of a philosophy dating to over 2,300 years ago in the age of its founder, Zeno, might have to offer to a twenty-first-century addict seeking a way to live sober, free, and happy. The first answer lies in the intensely therapeutic nature of Roman Stoicism. Epictetus is the man who coined the term "psychiatrist," meaning "soul doctor"; and he called his philosophy school "The Hospital" (*iatreion*). Roman Stoicism has always been a philosophy of psychic change, in fact precisely the type of psychic change that the Twelve-Step programs declare one must experience to remain drug or alcohol free. Unlike many philosophies both ancient and modern that might be viewed, justly or unjustly, as primarily interested in contemplating sometimes abstruse questions, Roman Stoicism is unquestionably dedicated to a way of life focusing all its attention on "transformation of character and consciousness." It is powerfully pragmatic and oriented to taking action to change one's life. In fact, both Albert Ellis and Aaron Beck, the two principal founders of Cognitive Behavioral Therapy, one of the therapeutic methods found to be most effective in changing one's thought patterns, cite the Stoics as the sources for their psychological theories.

A second advantage lies in the nonreligious nature of the Stoic conception of a Higher Power. For the many addicts and alcoholics who have a deep aversion to religion, the language invoking deity and the Judeo-Christian ethics woven into the thread of the "Big Book" of *Alcoholics Anonymous*, the text that is the model for most other Twelve-Step addiction recovery programs, have long been stumbling blocks. Some have found their way around these issues, but many turned away precisely because of this content. The beauty of a Stoic philosophical track to the kind of spiritual and psychological development required for recovery from addiction is its basis in logical and analytical thinking divorced from religious associations. For the Stoics, whose guiding power in the universe was interchangeably known as the *logos* ("rationality/reason"), *phusis* ("nature"), or *theos* ("god") in Greek, or perhaps best, *ratio naturae* ("the reason/rationality of the natural universe") in Latin, the acceptance of a nondogmatic spirituality is inherent to their philosophical perspective. Adoption of such a perspective can aid the atheist or agnostic in dealing with the unattractive religious aspects of Twelve-Step recovery programs.

The third way in which Roman Stoicism is very apt as a source of spiritual guidance in the life of the recovering addict is the nature of the source material itself. Unlike Plato, Aristotle, Epicurus, Lucretius, and many other ancient philosophers, Epictetus, Marcus Aurelius, and Seneca often present their spiritual wisdom in concise, easily digestible meditation formats rather than in dialogues or treatises, letters, or epic poems. In other words, it is rather easy to begin incorporating inspirational Stoic readings alongside the standard meditation, contemplation, and reflection texts of recovery, such as the Hazelden meditation series or the various AA readers such as *Daily Reflections*.

A fourth reason why Stoicism may speak well to today's recovering person is that we happen to find ourselves in a kind of neo-Stoic Renaissance, generally speaking. As I write this, I can click onto *Esquire* magazine's Lifestyle section and see that it features a brief article entitled, "I Was Lost Until I Become a Stoic." Ryan Holiday has proliferated popularized tidbits of Stoic wisdom in prepackaged formats in his *Daily Stoic*. While as a professional Classicist focused on Hellenistic philosophy and Stoicism in particular, I take some issue with the methodologies of these popular "hot takes" on Stoicism, one cannot deny that the culture has taken a bit of a turn to demystifying Stoicism. If such a cultural undercurrent helps the reader approach more serious and in-depth engagement with Stoicism, then it is for the good in the end. Perhaps a Holiday leads a reader to real philosophers like Pigliucchi or Irvine, and books that apply Stoicism to life in a more systematic and deeper way, like Hadot's *Philosophy as a Way of Life* or this book here.

The plan of this book is to allow one of the three chief Roman Stoics—Epictetus, Seneca, and Marcus Aurelius—to guide the reader through six aspects of recovery from alcoholism. In doing so, these guides will be discussed alongside their respective Twelve-Step suggestions, providing philosophical and psychological depth to the recovery injunctions. All translations from the original Greek or Latin are my best attempts at conveying as literally as idiom allows the philosophical import of the original texts.

I wish to thank the following:

Phillip Mitsis, whose seminar on Lucretius at Princeton University over twenty-five years ago first kindled in me an interest in Hellenistic philosophy that would deepen throughout my academic career and, more importantly, my life. It would lead me in time to the particular spiritual discipline founded around the teachings of the Roman Stoics and the wisdom of Alcoholics Anonymous of which this book is a product.

Greg Tobin, who served as a prudent helmsman for the navigation of the publishing world, and Gracie C., who knew he was the man for me to talk to.

My AA sponsors over the years of my recovery: Jeff C., Charlie M., Ernie B., Mark C., and especially Don C.

All my students throughout the years who endured all my talk of the Stoics, especially my Seneca seminar in Scottsdale, Arizona, in 2023. It was while teaching this class that I first conceived the idea for this book.

Raica Tarr, a Latin student of a few years ago, who did the amazing drawing of Marcus Aurelius found on the cover here.

My home base for writing, the back porch (naturally, for the Stoics) of The Snowshoe Hare, perched on the Big Spring Fork in the Monongehela National Forest in Slatyfork, West Virginia, and Kelsie, who kept me supplied with fruit smoothies to fuel the writing process there.

Richard Brown, Victoria Shi, Talia Hudgins, Darcy Ahl, and the rest of the folks at Bloomsbury for helping the book become what it is.

1

Epictetus on Breaking the Habit

The Path to a Personal *Askesis*

Of the myriad issues facing the addict attempting to find their footing in recovery, perhaps none is more fundamental than the search for a substitute to their old routine of procuring their drug of choice and then spending night and day thinking about using said substance. Alcoholics Anonymous wisely addresses this issue through the focus on meeting attendance for the newcomer, highly recommending that the newly dry alcoholic attend ninety meetings in ninety days, thus establishing a substitute pattern in place of their drinking. As the newly sober person establishes this pattern, they learn through both meetings and the working of the Twelve Steps of other routines that are strongly suggested as daily practices for the cultivation of serenity, emotion regulation, and the building of spiritual defenses against picking up a drink. These include but are not limited to meditation (i.e., Eleventh Step) and inventory taking (i.e., Tenth Step) concerning the thoughts and feelings of a given day. These two practices are often recommended as the beginning and the ending, respectively, to any given day—thus bookending the waking hours with an opening and closing acknowledgment of the principal position recovery must occupy in one's life as well as producing a change in thought patterns through consistent practice.

The Roman Stoic Epictetus (*c.* 50 CE–135 CE) is a most natural and harmonious guide to explaining and enriching the practices of early recovery, as he is Western philosophy's foremost thinker on *askesis*, the training of one's thoughts through rigorous philosophical reflection and the practice of certain habits of mind. Part of what makes Epictetus' exhortations so vivid is his depiction of his philosophy students undergoing this training as athletes beginning a new regimen.[1] Through this analogy Epictetus "coaches up" his students and reaches us, the modern reader, in search of moral improvement in newly addiction-free lives, through an accessible set of easily recognizable ideas.

What is it, then, that Epictetus can add as moral psychology coach alongside the AA program? As a clear, concise, and rigorously rational philosopher he provides to those seeking it further explication of both the reasons and contexts for their practices of recovery. Epictetus can not only help coach the recovering person alongside their AA coaches, but additionally provide a fully realized, rational account of why such a program is necessitated, how it works, and most importantly, how it fits into an entire *ars vita*. This is the Roman term for an "art of life" and the phrase by which Hellenistic philosophers understood themselves to be offering to their students not philosophy as an academic subject, but a true handbook on how to live well.[2]

Recovery as *Agon* and the Path to Agonistic Self-Mastery

Let us first consider how Epictetus may help us conceptualize the struggle of recovery in the language of his philosophical athletic training. Epictetus consistently refers to life as an *agon*, or "contest." In what sense is life a contest? And for what?

> For the greatest *contest*[3] must not be shrunk from by those contesting, rather the blows must be taken: For the contest which lies in front of you is not in wrestling or the pankration,[4] in which it is possible for the man winning or losing to be a man of great or little value, or, even by Zeus, for him to be a fortunate or unhappy man, but rather this is a contest for good fortune and happiness itself.
>
> (Arr. *Epict.* 3.25.2–3) (All translations are mine)

Life for Epictetus is a contest akin to a combat sport, in that one faces not just the physical challenge of any sport but also violence directed at them by an opponent. Addicts may readily identify with such imagery, often speaking in terms of themselves versus the disease (which is, after all, part of themselves), or wrestling with the monkey on their back, or fighting a kind of Mr. Hyde version of themselves with their recovering Dr. Jekyll. But for what does Epictetus believe his Stoic students are fighting, and how is this fight akin to that of recovering individuals facing off against their addictions? Epictetus' contest of life is for the achievement of permanent psychical freedoms: freedom from irrational passions that seek to overwhelm a person's life through embracing dispassionate acceptance (*apatheia*), freedom from fortune and its caprice (*eleutheria*), and freedom from mental disturbance (*ataraxia*). These are the components of true Stoic *eudaimonia*, or "happiness." In Twelve-Step recovery the focus is likewise on a "psychic change," which leads to freedom from the substance and then, with spiritual growth over time, a deeper freedom that speaks to every aspect of the recovering person's life in much the same terms as the Stoic teacher to his students. In AA the goal is often described as "living happy, joyous, and free."

Freedom is, of course, a central theme of Stoic ethics and never more so than in Epictetus' particular brand of Stoicism. But who is our opponent as recovering persons in the contest but an enslaved version of our very selves? And so it is for Epictetus that to achieve *apatheia*, *eleutheria*, and *ataraxia*, one must master oneself in the contest by defeating one's baser inclinations and overcoming daily psychological challenges. This agonistic self-mastery, the defeating of one's addict self in the contest, is an apt description of the recovery process.[5] The victory of recovery is a serene sense of command over what is within one's sphere of control and a letting go of what isn't. The Stoic version of this leads us to their definition of the function of human virtue more generally: dispassionate rational action free of anger and fear, resentment and impatience. Overcoming these very same negative emotions is also the focus of the Twelve Steps. For the Stoic, fighting these passions is the contest for virtue and thus happiness.

It is indeed quite a rigorous training that is needed to prepare for the contest in which an individual may be victorious in this achievement. But Epictetus has good news for all of us in this regard. By keeping his focus upon the *prokopton* figure, or "person making progress," in line with most of the Middle Stoics and those who followed them,[6] Epictetus makes it clear that we may lose the contest many times, so long as we retain our willingness to step back into the fray with ourselves:

> What then? Even if we shall fail here, no one forbids us from contesting again nor is it necessary to wait another four-year period, so that another Olympia comes around, but rather right away it is possible for the one having recovered himself and bringing the same zeal to contest: even if you should again yield, it is possible again to compete, and if you may achieve victory one time, you will be like one never having yielded.
>
> (Arr. *Epict.* 3.25.4)

There are no external blocks to our efforts at progress toward victory. Only we can prevent ourselves. Here is true freedom from fortune. Epictetus chooses to emphasize here the part of the metaphor that does not, in fact, fit. The philosophical athlete need not wait for another contest to come around. The contest remains ever before us—in fact, within us.[7] Happiness for Epictetus is not a state of being resulting from a wide variety of external factors, but rather a difficult level of self-mastery to be achieved by rigorous training, persistent effort, and a determination to persevere in the face of setbacks. It is a disposition to always wish to compete against one's lesser self and to get up off the mat after defeat or failure.[8] Setbacks, defeats, and the like are challenges that offer opportunities for analysis and self-improvement for the next contest. It is a mindset up to the individual since it concerns progress rather than attainment. It is a disposition rather than a state.

Herein lies an encouraging message for the recovering addict who may well stumble a few times before finding their footing in a program of recovery. In fact, on my anecdotal survey from ten plus years listening in meetings, the majority of alcoholics with long-term recovery of five years or more stumbled a few times, and sometimes quite a bit more than a few times, before finding sobriety. The "stick and stay" alcoholic, a person who stayed sober from their very first meeting, is a relative rarity in AA. Additionally, the focus of the Roman Stoics on progress is in accord with another recovery mantra, "progress over perfection."

Habituation: *Askesis* "Training" over *Ethos* "Habit"

As Epictetus' Stoic insights help to conceptualize both the struggle and the aims of recovery, it is really in the "how" of recovery that he has the most to offer to the recovering person. The Stoics, and Epictetus in particular, were master theorists and practitioners of habituation and its import in changing one's life. How one lives is, in Greek philosophy, their *ethos*. As Aristotle first formulated it, one's *ethos* is the product of habits. Stoic *askesis*, on the other hand, is more deliberate training than mere habituation; thus it may be termed "intentional habituation."[9] Consider for a moment in the light of early recovery Becker's description of the Stoic conception of behavioral dispositions, *ethoi*, in relation to mere habits of Aristotle: "behavioral dispositions were supposed to arise through (or at least, in the mature agent, be brought under the control of) the process of habituation—a process in which deliberate, conscious choice becomes routinized, nondeliberative, habitual conduct."[10] Habit does not carry the necessary weight of the Stoic construction of *ethos* as defined here. And it would be a vast underplaying of the effort needed for recovery to reduce the process to a change of habits. Intentional habituation is, rather, training, discipline, and exercise. This is the goal of the ninety meetings in ninety days, a very frequent injunction disguised as a suggestion alongside several others for newcomers such as: daily meditation, nightly inventory, daily phone calls to one's sponsor, etc. I myself managed seventy-seven meetings in my first ninety days without the use of a car, and though I regretted not making the recommended ninety, I felt the benefits of the seventy-seven. Alcoholics Anonymous members often speak of having "smart feet," meaning that through deliberative routine they found themselves at a meeting when a particular emotional experience of the day—often the very resentment, anger, fear, or impatience that Epictetus himself discusses—was pushing them in the direction of a drink. AAs also frequently talk about meetings as the place they come to "build their sobriety muscles." The understanding of recovery as a training process allows the recovering person to delve with Epictetus deeper into the *askesis* through the analogy of athletic training.

The "Serenity Prayer" and Epictetus' Dichotomy of Control

Victor La Cerva, MD, a very insightful modern philosopher of recovery, offers the following perspective in one of his books of daily meditations for recovery:

> Changing a habit is always based on reaching toward the new rather than rejecting the old. Automatic routines and behaviors remain flexible throughout our life—we are not powerless before them! We know from our own experience that the Twelve Step principles comprise a really ginormous, successful awareness mechanism for shifting habits.[11]

The establishment of a new routine to replace the life of drinking is up to us. The disease of alcoholism is not up to us. We are powerless over the drink once it has entered our body. This is the powerlessness of Step One in the Twelve Steps. We are not powerless about making a choice to turn our life over to the Higher Power of AA recovery. Epictetus' *askesis* broadens and deepens through his philosophical perspective many of the key components of the Twelve Steps and the further principles of Alcoholics Anonymous.

Let us begin with perhaps most widely known thing about AA, its use of the "Serenity Prayer":

> God, grant me the serenity to accept the things I cannot
> change, the courage to change the things I can,
> and the wisdom to know the difference.[12]

The opening selection of Epictetus' *Encheiridion* expresses the same philosophical idea in clear lecture form rather than as a prayer:

> Some of the things are up to us, while others are not up to us. Up to us are conception, choice, desire, aversion, and in a word, everything that is our own doing; not up to us are our body, our property, reputation, office, and in a word, everything that is not our doing.
>
> (*Encheiridion* 1.1)

Epictetus' elucidation of what is and isn't under our control sets up the external/internal dichotomy so central to Stoic ethics, echoed in recovery talk by the familiar "all my problems exist in the six inches between my ears" or similar phrases. The Stoic dichotomy provides clarity to the alcoholic's situation at all stages of recovery, but for now let us focus on the beginning of one's sober journey.[13] In the beginning there is the seemingly uncontrollable yearning of body and mind for the missing substance. But within our power is a choice to take a turn away from the liquor store toward a building where a meeting is being held. That choice was the most difficult one most recovering individuals say they ever had to make. Epictetus is anything but oblivious to this. It is precisely because it is so simple yet so extraordinarily difficult that he expends so much philosophical energy in categorizing and describing the two separate worlds of "things up to us" and "things not up to us" and then exhorting his students to focus exclusively on developing the skills to work on those that are up to us.

Askesis and *Apatheia:* "Freedom from Emotional Suffering"

Having now a picture of what the *agon* of life is and what victory in it means for Epictetus, let us examine his concept of the true athlete and the kind of training he imagines his philosophical athletes to be undertaking. Of primary importance to this training is a singular focus on the most fundamental ground of Epictetus' ethical system: the question of what is and what isn't up to us as human agents.[14] For Epictetus all psychological disturbance in life arises from one root cause: the wishing and wanting for things external to oneself to be other than they, in fact, are.[15] The alcoholic's dilemma is identical in that, as Bill Wilson states in *Alcoholics Anonymous*, they seek to control that which they are, in fact, utterly powerless over: "The idea that somehow, someday he will control and enjoy his drinking is the great obsession of every abnormal drinker."[16] Only with true acceptance of their powerlessness can the alcoholic hope to move forward; and that acceptance arrives with a true understanding of what is up to them and what isn't. This singular essential focus, that with proper discernment of what is and isn't up to you, you will be able to live so that nothing comes out contrary to what you want, and nothing will happen that you don't wish for, is the cornerstone of Epictetus' system. Through embracing this understanding, *apatheia*, *eleutheria*, and *ataraxia* can be attained. Epictetus wants a student prepared to be an athlete of this:

> Give me one young man having come into school with this same point of view, one becoming an athlete of this matter and saying

> that "As far as I'm concerned, be gone with all the rest, it is sufficient for me if it is possible to lead a life free from interference and free from grief and to stretch forth my neck to the affairs of life as one free to look up to the heavens as a friend of God fearing nothing which is able to come to pass." (Arr. *Epict.* 2.17.29–30)

It is the focus on freedom, in varied aspects, that Epictetus emphasizes. This freedom is available through becoming an athlete of dispassionate acceptance known to the Stoics as *apatheia.*

Learning Stoic Acceptance: *Apatheia*

Apatheia is the singular most important aim of Stoic ethics and the key to happiness, or *eudaimonia.* To accept things as they truly are without unnecessary emotional vexation is to align one's individual rational faculty with that of the universe. For the alcoholic, this entails the embracing of one's alcoholism as a defining fact of one's existential identity. To recover is to know both that one cannot drink like other people and to know that one's alcoholic past has warped the psychological and emotional response systems of body and mind. Without the substance to turn to in circumstances of stress the alcoholic must learn from the ground up how to respond rather than reflexively react. Here again Epictetus' detailed elucidation of the path to *apatheia* for his Stoic students offers the recovering individual reasoned and practical methods of progress.

The first key in progressing toward *apatheia* is becoming more deft in handling *phantasiai*, the impressions that evoke emotional reactions from us in the world. These constitute our reactions to events prior to rational reflection, and they are the source of the passions that can destroy our humanity, namely anger, erotic lust, hatred, and fear.[17] The agonistic life of the Epictetan Stoic is a daily wrestling match against the impact of these *phantasiai*. The true Stoic exercises themself against these; and they are the true athlete, the true practitioner of *askesis*:

> This one exercising himself against such impressions is the one trainee in athletics.
>
> (Arr. *Epict.* 2.18.27)

This exercise is what has the lasting effects on the recovering person's life. Davidson states, "We become a different type of person, not because we willed or decided upon a different life, but because we submitted to different practices that inexorably reshape the ethical athlete."[18] The Epictetan Stoic treats these impressions like a wrestling or boxing opponent, feeling them out carefully, assessing their strengths and weaknesses, and evaluating how best to defeat them.[19] Epictetus paints a vivid portrait of this wrestling match:

> But rather put some other beautiful and noble impression against it and throw out the filthy one. And if you habituate yourself to exercise in such fashion, you will see what your shoulders will become like, what your sinews, what your tensile force: now you are building mere words and not one thing more.
>
> (Arr. *Epict.* 2.18.25)

In order to lessen the emotional impact of a particular impression on ourselves, Epictetus wants us to set up a competing and opposite impression. The result of such exercise is the moral strength matching visible strength in the athlete's shoulders, sinews, and tensile force, visible in the philosophy student in their choices of how to live. If the impression comes upon you that those who possess great wealth are fortunate, oppose this impression with consideration of the troubles inherent to being rich, such as the pleas of friends for a loan, the time spent managing property and goods that could be better invested in further training toward the goals of *apatheia*, *eleutheria*, and *ataraxia*. If an impression is too much for you at your level of training, avoid it.[20] You are not yet ready for the contest, as Epictetus makes clear in discussing the unequal combat between a beautiful woman and the novice student of philosophy.[21] These do not harmonize, like a beautiful piece of pottery and a stone. Wise elders of AA frequently advise newly recovering individuals to assiduously avoid situations where strong impressions might trigger the craving for a drink. This could mean simply not entering bars; but it might also entail avoiding dating in early recovery as drinking is such a common means of loosening up in first-date scenarios. In fact, for AA newcomers it is strongly suggested that they not make any big changes during the first year of recovery. Moving, starting or ending an intimate relationship, changing careers, and other highly stressful and potentially triggering life changes are seen by experienced AAs as the contests for which the newcomer is more than likely not yet ready.

The application of a competing and opposite impression in the contest of recovery is one of the core practices in progressing toward dispassionate acceptance. To the thought that alcoholics frequently entertain of the unfairness of their disease, oppose consideration of suffering from other ailments that are deadlier and without solution.

Thinking along these lines for a bit may lead one to wisdom expressed in the idea that if everyone in a meeting were to toss their problems toward the center of the table like a set of car keys, most people would prefer to leave with their own problems rather than exchange them for those of their fellow meeting attendees.[22]

Related is certainly one of the most common practices advocated in recovery: the composing of a gratitude list. If the impression comes upon you that your alcoholism has cost you the job in which you felt most fulfilled, oppose it with consideration of how your newfound freedom from drink opens a wide variety of possibilities for fulfilling employment that your drink-enslaved self may never have even considered. Many alcoholics as they progress in recovery find jobs that they would never have been led to without the loss of their previous careers. And many state that these jobs are more rewarding than those they left behind.

The Recovery Odds and the Beauty of the Difficult for a Stoic

Addiction specialists in psychology, psychiatry, and clinical rehabilitation counseling often cite the disheartening odds against long-term recovery from addiction and/or alcoholism in many places in the recovery literature. While reliable numbers can be hard to come by with the involvement of factors such as anonymity, the challenges of tracking people over decades, and the common pattern for many of multiple relapses before finding sobriety, the proximity of the estimates pulled from a variety of sources suggests that while it is quite possible to recover from what *Alcoholics Anonymous* terms "a seemingly hopeless state of mind and body,"[23] it is very far from easy, and in terms of odds quite simply significantly less than likely. Most estimates put the percentage of alcoholics achieving long-term continuous sobriety, defined as five years or longer, between 8 and 12 percent. I vividly recall a counselor at my inpatient rehabilitation center telling the 140 newly dry persons seated in the room that 3 of us were likely to put together five years of continuous sobriety.[24] While some may question the effect such truth-telling has on those trying to find their way in recovery, Epictetus would urge us to accept the facts of the extreme challenge of recovery as an opportunity.

Epictetus would prefer to have his trainees fully aware of just what they are up against. He pulls no punches regarding the challenge of the training he is calling his students to set out upon. He imagines a conversation between himself as trainer and a young man who declares his desire to win an Olympic victory. He suggests that most people do not take sufficient consideration of the discipline and hardship a commitment to such a goal requires. The athlete must abide by a strict diet, train in heat and cold, at whatever time is prescribed by his trainer.[25] But even adherence to intensive training is no guarantee of success in the contest itself:

> Still in the contest you must dig in one against the other; there will be times when you may dislocate your wrist, turn your ankle, swallow a lot of sand, be whipped: and after all this it is still possible that you will sometimes be conquered. Reckoning up these things, if you still wish, set out to be an athlete.
>
> (Arr. *Epict.* 3.15.4)

Only when you have carefully reckoned your willingness to endure the pains of the fight and potential defeat should you declare yourself ready. Epictetus insists that you must become willing to grow out of being a child who likes to play at being an athlete at one time, a gladiator at another, and a musician at a third.[26] Commitment is singular in the same way as ethical focus. Notably, this entire section on the athletic training analogy recurs in the *Readers' Digest* version of Epictetus' philosophy, "The Manual," *Encheiridion* 29, emphasizing the central focus this analogy plays in illuminating Epictetus' philosophy of life.

Those who have found success in recovery frequently emphasize many of the same ethical points as Epictetus does here. Commitment to recovery must take priority in one's life as training for an athlete aiming at the Olympics. All else in life must top out at second position at the highest, be it job, marriage, children, or anything else. Discipline and hardship are ways of life for the person attempting to get sober and for those who have found their way to long-term recovery. Daily meditations, which are never or nearly never skipped, are a form of discipline frequently mentioned in meetings. Meeting attendance itself is perhaps the most visible form of AA discipline. The person attempting their ninety meetings in ninety days often sees the same faces in those early days, the faces of people with eight, fifteen, twenty-two, or thirty-three years of continuous sobriety. These middle- and long-timers, often queried by friends and family as to why they continue to attend meetings so often after so many years away from a drink, are accustomed to smile and say something along the lines of how a diabetic wouldn't give up taking insulin.

Early recovery features for many alcoholics the kind of defeat described by Epictetus in the passage above. Despite the endurance of much hardship and suffering, the disease often still, hopefully temporarily, wins the day. But like the wrestler, the boxer, and *pankratiast* or "mixed martial artist," we can come back from such a setback, more determined than ever:

> But learn from the gymnastic trainers. The trainee has suffered a fall: "Stand up, he says, wrestle again, until you make yourself strong."
>
> (Arr. *Epict.* 4.9.15–16)

But unlike the pugilistic athlete, who may in the end fight an opponent whom he can never defeat, the internal *agon* is decided within ourselves:

> For within oneself are both destruction and the cure.
>
> (Arr. *Epict.* 4.9.16–17)

Let us reflect a bit more deeply on the *agon* with the self as portrayed in the athletic analogy and its application to addiction recovery through the perspective of a modern Stoic, the philosopher William Irvine. Irvine, who adopted Stoicism and a vigorous rowing regimen at about the same time in his life, frames the agonistic confrontation with self in clearly athletic terms:

> When I row competitively, it may look as though I am trying to beat the other rowers, but I am in fact engaged in a much more significant competition: the one against my other self. He didn't want to learn to row. He didn't want to do workouts, preferring instead to spend the predawn hours asleep in a warm bed.
>
> (Irvine 2009, 264)

For Irvine, Epictetus' athletic analogy is now a homology; the same principles that guide him ethically govern his athletic discipline. Many alcoholics do not want to get sober, just as Irvine did not want to get out of his comfortable bed. They may know they need to get sober in order to stay alive and live well, just as Irvine knew exercise was a vital part of living and living well. But the other self had to be overcome.

Epictetus tells us that we ought to embrace the opportunity of facing such a difficult opponent as our addict selves. The only way we can strengthen ourselves for the contest is by training with difficult opponents. As Pleket succinctly summarizes it, "Epictetus" training above all is concerned with *ta duskataponeta* ("things that are difficult to master").[27] In the sphere of the analogy from training for combat athletics things that are difficult to master appear as particularly fit and capable adversaries. As the skilled training partner readies one physically, so certain difficult to master people and situations exercise us in the Stoic virtues:

> What benefit does the trainer provide the athlete? The greatest. This man [i.e., the one who abuses me] becomes my trainer: He exercises my tolerance, my restraint from anger, my mild manner.
>
> (Arr. *Epict.* 3.20.9)

The difficult person in your life is an opportunity for training, not an obstacle.[28] Bad neighbors are bad for themselves but good for us, according to Epictetus. They provide an opportunity to assess our progress in tolerance, patience, restraint, and lack of resentment.[29] These qualities for "dealing with life on life's terms" as the AA saying puts it, are ethical pillars of recovery. The alcoholic personality is plagued by intolerance and impatience, lack of restraint, and deep resentment, which *Alcoholics Anonymous* deems the "'number one" offender,[30] meaning the emotional experience most likely to push an alcoholic toward a drink. The reasons for the alcoholic's difficulty in dealing with the difficult things in life are traceable to their turn away from productive tools for handling situations toward the escape of chemical alteration. How much better, in that case, does Epictetus' training regimen suit the alcoholic than even the average person? The struggle of the first few years of recovery is often centered on learning how to handle the difficult things in life without turning back to the drink. A sentiment I have heard many an alcoholic with years of recovery under their belt share in meetings is that without the challenge of their alcoholism, without their alcoholic self to contend against, they never could have achieved the kind of patience, tolerance, restraint, and freedom from resentment they now enjoy in their lives. It was only through wrangling with the toughest of opponents that they came out so well-trained. The unironic, truly sincere use of the self-identification "grateful alcoholic," a term that often mystifies newer recovering addicts and nonaddicts alike, arises out of this recognition of the ultimate value of the contest.

All of this makes clear sense when reflected through the athletic training analogy again. No athlete trying to improve would ever request an easy opponent, knowing that nothing can be gained from matching oneself against an inferior in strength and skill or in coasting through an easy training regimen. The serious athlete yearns for the most difficult opponent they can reasonably hope to contend with and the most intense training regimen they can handle in order to perform a self-assessment of their progress. A life of ease is a life without the opportunity for moral progress:

> Difficulties are the things which reveal men for who they are. Well then, whenever a difficulty befalls you, remember that god, like a trainer in the gymnasium, has matched you against a rugged young man. For what purpose? In order that you become an Olympic champion. It does not happen without sweat. No one seems to me to possess a better difficulty than the one which you have, so long as you are willing to make use of it as an athlete does a young opponent.
>
> (Arr. *Epict.* 1.24.1–2)

The difficulties of life are for Epictetus training challenges set us by our trainer, god or reason, in order that we may achieve a great victory in life. Pigliucci, another modern Stoic of insight, concludes: "In a sort of life judo, the Stoic faces up to adversity by treating life itself as a wrestler in the training ring, as an opponent who is not (necessarily) out to beat us, but whose purpose is to keep us on our toes; the Stoic becomes eager to face his opponent because that's the way toward self-improvement."[31] Approaching the foundation of a philosophy of life built for recovery as an athlete would is Epictetus' prescription. Only by making use of difficulties like sparring partners can we hope to progress toward the true freedoms of *apatheia*, *eleutheria*, and *ataraxia*.

Showing Progress: "Walking the Walk" of Recovery

"Progress over perfection" is one of the most frequently heard mantras of recovery. The focus on progress in Twelve-Step recovery is perfectly aligned with the Roman Stoics. From the time of the Stoic Panaetius (*c.* 185 BCE–*c.*110 BCE) onward, there was a significant shift in focus from the contemplation of the figure of the perfected wise man, *sapiens,* as moral exemplar to comparison with one's own former self as an evaluation of progress. Within the athletic analogy Epictetus insists on seeing results, not fancy training equipment, from his philosophical athletes:

> Therefore show me your progress here. For just as if I should say to an athlete "show me your shoulders," and then that man said, "look at my dumbbells." "Look to, you and your weights." I want to see the results of your dumbbells.
>
> (Arr. *Epict.* 1.4.13)

Epictetus here again focuses on progress in one's training but emphasizes that the results must be outwardly apparent. The athlete cannot take their trainer to the gym, show them thousands of dollars in the latest training equipment and gadgetry, and hope to claim progress.[32] Likewise, the philosophical athlete can't show off their adeptness with handling syllogisms and hope to impress Epictetus. The athlete displays their change through their physique and performance. The philosophical athlete shows the progress they have made in three critical aspects of Stoic moral theory: pursuits and avoidances, desires and aversions, and assent to and dissent from impressions. All three of these are dependent on the fitness of the *hegemonikon*, the ruling rational faculty's ability to harmonize itself with the *ratio naturae*, as the Romans called it, or, as Epictetus frames it, acting *sumphonos te phusei* ("being yourself in harmony with nature"). As the combat athlete's training is obvious in the formation of their back and shoulders with which they engage their opponent, so Epictetus asks to witness the change in his student's *hegemonikon*:

> But from these things imparted to you show some change in your own governing rational faculty, as athletes do their shoulders from the exercise they've done and from what they've eaten, as those having learned a craft by heart from what they have acquired knowledge of.
>
> (Arr. *Epict.* 3.21.3)

The growth of our *apatheia*, *eleutheria*, and *ataraxia* can be demonstrated by our wrestling or boxing with our desires and aversions, pursuits and avoidances, and assents and dissents, becoming more flexible and agile. These are the clear proofs of our *hegemonikon*'s increased athleticism, just us the shoulders of the wrestler or boxer are for the combat athlete.

What proofs of progress does the recovering alcoholic look for in themself? What proofs do others observe in them? Similar to Epictetus' contempt for philosophy students who excel at logical quibbles and syllogisms is the disdain old-timers in AA have for relative newcomers who wield a great fluency with the language of the program and recovery more generally. As one of the other most common mantras has it, "AA is a program of action." Speaking fluently of their addiction struggle when just returning from yet another relapse is seen as equivalent to Epictetus' imagined interlocutor who wants to show their fancy new weight training equipment but has little or no muscle to show for it. On the other hand, those with a long and fertile recovery will often point out someone who is truly "walking the walk" and not just "talking the talk" of recovery in living by the principles of AA and cultivating a deeper spiritual life, through Christianity, Buddhism, Stoicism, or another supplemental tradition of spiritual enlightenment of their own choosing by inclination or acculturation.

Stoic Self-Evaluation and AA Inventory Work

Epictetus' insistence that we become philosophical athletes provides a lens through which to look deeper into some of the core concepts and larger issues of Stoic moral theory and practice and its relevance to recovery. Stoic self-evaluation should prove a good starting point as it maps neatly onto the Tenth Step and through this the Fourth Step as well.

Stoicism with its continual emphasis on moral progress being an inside job is particularly concerned that we be hypervigilantly self-aware through a discipline of self-evaluative processes. As Nussbaum states it:

> Part of the sluggishness and carelessness of everyday life as it is normally lived is its failure completely to grasp its own experiences and deeds, its failure to recognize and take stock of itself. The Stoic idea of learning is an idea of increasing vigilance and wakefulness, as the mind, increasingly rapid and alive, learns to repossess its own experiences from the fog of habit, convention, and forgetfulness.
>
> (Nussbaum 1994, 340)

This repossession of the self requires a particular kind of perspective on volition that views our will as subordinated to a psychological and spiritual practice. Epictetan *askesis* requires, as Davidson formulates it, "treating one's volition as a quasi-object to be adjusted through practical techniques."[33] Epictetus' philosophical athlete is never sluggish or careless in their approach to training, treating themself as an object of training, not a person with the "free will" to declare they do not feel like training today.[34] Athletes must continuously log their training sessions and take stock of their progress, make adjustments, and shock the body out of physiological torpor brought on by excessive routine. They cannot expect real progress of any kind simply by showing up at the gymnasium and going through habituated motions. Various studies have shown how a large percentage of regular gymgoers never really make any kind of progress because of this default to the habitual. Nussbaum further speaks in terms of the "assiduous daily litigation" the Stoic undergoes when they step away from the world for a session of self-evaluation.[35] Epictetus asks us to think of the same process as a mental shadow-boxing in which we learn from the weakness of our own default movements and compensate for them. The shadow-boxing mind is vigilant, quick, focused, agile, and adaptable.

Taking stock of one's own actions and mind is a central part of Twelve-Step recovery. Most specifically, it is through the practice of the Tenth Step—"continued to take personal inventory and when we were wrong promptly admitted it," the daily present-day version of the retrospective moral inventory work done in the Fourth Step—that the alcoholic performs the process of "assiduous daily litigation." Most AAs with time in the program practice a nightly inventory through which they analyze their emotional experience in relation to their behavior in their interactions with others and themselves. In this way one endeavors to take possession of one's experience. Perhaps there is a coworker who pushes your buttons, leading to resentment and frustration. The Tenth-Step practice asks one to examine why you feel this way, how you treat this person, and, most importantly, to contemplate how absurd it is that this person has such control of your mind. What the Stoic adds is how to make this recovery practice part of a more rigorous training of the mind toward awareness, self-possession, rationality, and agency.

Additionally, as any AA with a good amount of time in recovery will be quick to point out, just showing up at meetings but not engaging in more in-depth psychic work might keep you from picking up a drink, but it won't lead you to freedom or happiness. This is the equivalent of the regular gymgoer who sees no results because they do not realize that the body adapts to the same routine repeated over and over without adjustment via challenge.

Stoic Agency and the Recovering Person's Sense of Personal Psychological Responsibility

One of the key terms in virtue ethics is "agency." Agency in the philosophical sense is the recognition by an individual of their actions as determining their own happiness or unhappiness with the corollary that no person or circumstance has the power to make one feel any particular way without that person allowing it. In Roman Stoic terms, agency denotes rational agency. Epictetus aims at increasing the fitness of his students in exercising their agency. Becker gives an account of agency that echoes Epictetus' approach:

> Physical fitness is the result of training a more or less healthy body to function especially well for a given purpose. The purpose may be the prevention of cardiovascular disease; the development of work-related abilities, athletic prowess, self-esteem, or beauty; the attempt to compensate for a disability, and so forth. Whatever the purpose, the training is designed to adjust the size, strength, flexibility, speed, skill, stability, or control of one's body well beyond the minimum required for physical health, up to a level of excellence or fitness for the purpose. Psychological fitness is analogous, and fitness in the case of agency proper is the result of increasing the scope, strength, speed, accuracy, stability, control, and effectiveness of one's powers of deliberation and choice—and of the traits constructed through the exercise of these powers—for practical purposes generally.
>
> (Becker 1998, 105)

Becker makes no mention of Epictetus specifically in his analysis of agency in his chapter on virtue in his book *A New Stoicism,* but it is difficult not to see a particularly Epictetan influence here. The progress toward ideal Stoic agency is for Becker a steady movement from health to fitness to virtuosity.[36] What is particularly noteworthy is the way in which the analogy to athletics in Becker's own terms is not fully apt for just any athletic endeavor, but rather especially suitable to combat athletics, boxing, or wrestling, Epictetus' own focal points. The adversarial or combat sports require a dedication to the development of the range of skills analogous to the psychological traits toward which Epictetus wishes his students to work.[37] In Epictetan terms, our *hegemonikon* must constantly undergo a wide array of training in order to make us better rational agents. Another way of framing the same Epictetan idea is to think about ethical training as, in Davidson's phrase, "the process of generating stronger internal compulsion."[38] To hand over the reins to the *hegemonikon*, our rational element, is to become true Stoic agents. This virtuosic agency is the one true goal or *telos* of Stoic ethics and the true nature of virtue in Stoicism.

What does the goal of virtuosic agency look like for the person in recovery? Internal compulsion, or "the treating of one's volition as a quasi-object," is a good place to start. As the repetition of rising early to engage in vigorous exercise generates an internal compulsion within the trainee to fight past the notion of hitting snooze on the alarm clock, so the conquering of the undermining thoughts "I just attended a meeting yesterday, so I'm fine" or "I'm too tired after work to get back up off this couch to drive all the way to a meeting" arises from having fought off the same thoughts on previous occasions. Repetition itself increases the likelihood of choosing correctly the next time. Anyone who has ever set foot in a gym knows there is a certain group of regulars seen every day, or every other day. These regulars never speak of getting back in shape or New Year's resolutions to drop twenty pounds. They talk of discipline and maintenance, training smart to avoid injury that would interrupt their routine, and fitness as a lifetime journey rather than a goal measured in pounds dropped or lifted. In other words, gymgoers who truly practice a Stoic *askesis* live their training in a fundamentally different way than others who go to the gym occasionally or for a specific time to lose a certain amount of weight. Many of those who find success in recovery, who learn to view their recovery from addiction not as the putting away of drugs or alcohol but as an ongoing process of psychological and spiritual development that takes abstinence as merely the beginning point of a more profound journey, share the same fundamental perspective.

Long-term AAs often employ techniques Epictetus would recognize and be pleased with. One of the methods of internal compulsion to meeting attendance is the oft-repeated "it's the meeting I don't feel like attending that I need to attend." This is a reminder that the will of the AA person is compelled by a previously made rational decision meant to counteract feelings in the moment. As in adhering to a workout plan, the AA person does the work of attending the "training session" that the meeting constitutes.

As meeting attendance is a practice in what to move toward, so AAs also practice temptation avoidance and situational awareness to produce an internal compulsion regarding what to move away from. Newly recovering alcoholics must not spend much time in bars or with friends who drink immoderately. To do so would be to invite temptation and forgetfulness about the reality of their alcoholism.

As it is framed in AA parlance, "Hang around at a barber shop long enough and you will get a haircut." Self-awareness for the alcoholic focuses in part on probable triggers, be they people, places, or things that ought to be avoided. This is akin to the athlete's practice of "weak-point training" wherein the athlete sets aside additional time in training those areas in which their skill and athleticism are least well-developed. Naturally, these weak points are where the athlete is more susceptible to injury as the recovery person's triggers point to where they are more vulnerable to running back to their substance of choice.

Apatheia as Stoic *Telos* and Serenity as Recovery Goal

Stoics are justly renowned, as well as frequently criticized and even mocked, for their conclusion that the exercise of virtuosic agency is happiness itself.[39] The contest for *eudaimonia* image with which I began this first chapter makes clear that for Epictetus *eudaimonia* is only accessible to one through a training that leads to *apatheia*, freedom from the passions. Stoicism frequently comes in for criticism at this juncture primarily because the true nature of Stoic *apatheia* is widely misunderstood. The emphasis on freedom from the passions has led many to conclude that living a Stoic life would entail either a particularly monk-like existence devoid of some of the most highly valued emotional experiences human life has to offer (e.g., romantic love) or a robotic, rational calculation lacking in humanity. The Stoic scholar Brad Inwood has corrected this misunderstanding of the emotional life of the Stoic by clarifying the Stoic position, showing that *apatheia* is *eupatheia*, or "good feeling," and "eupatheia is simply the impulse of a fully rational man."[40] Freedom from the passions is the good feeling, a kind of joy permeating all aspects of life. The Stoic will aim at the extirpation of all excessive emotions, some of which we might be inclined to believe difficult to live without. It is inconceivable to envision meaningful moral training without sacrifice of some kind. Just as the boxer must leave behind family and friends to focus on training camp, the Stoic recognizes certain costs associated with the progress toward virtuosic agency. As Becker argues, simply because a Stoic is "psychologically equipped to be detached and unfeeling"[41] does not imply that they always are. They remain in this state when it is required of them, just as the boxer is in a heightened state of readiness during training camp. In turn, the boxer can indulge in some junk food and lounging during the vacation after the big fight.

One way in which the Stoics approach the question of happiness seems particularly apt to Epictetus' focus on athleticism. Stoic theory argues that virtue is a stochastic craft; that is, one that concerns itself with aims rather than outcomes.[42] As Striker observes, this view of virtue has clear parallels with sports and games for "the intended result of winning the race is indifferent compared with the physical performance: the runner who loses the race has built up his strength just as much as the winner."[43] In fact, the most well-known image for the stochastic nature of virtue and happiness in Stoicism is one drawn from athletics, namely Cicero's portrait of the archer who recognizes that all good rests in his aiming at the target and that hitting the target qualifies as a preferred indifferent.[44] Hitting the target is not the archer's *telos*, or ultimate goal. Rather, it is the fulfillment of the craft of archery, everything that goes into being an archer and aiming as well as one's training and circumstances allow.[45] A gust of wind or the sudden moving of the target are things that lie outside of the craft of archery, things that are not up to the archer. Clearly, Epictetus views our engagement in the contest for happiness in just these terms. We have performed as good Epictetan Stoics so long as we have trained assiduously and been willing to engage in combat. If we lose, we have not failed the craft of virtue, as we will have made moral progress. The only way to really lose is to refuse to keep training or become unwilling to enter the combat again. A Stoic can only lose by failing in the training phase by the mismanagement of *phantasiai*, or impressions. Stochastically speaking, the greatest fight you ever fight might be a losing one, but it would lack nothing in terms of virtue and thus happiness if the fight is, in fact, the greatest exercise of the fullest realization of your *hegemonikon*'s rational capacities for selection and thus your moral capabilities. The boxer can exercise the most perfected form of their agency and still lose.[46] Their focus should be on self-measurement by their own agency.[47] In light of this it should not be surprising that a few of the most exemplary Stoic heroes are people who fail and choose death after their last and greatest fight, which resulted in a virtuous defeat. How can Socrates or Cato be thought to have lacked anything of virtue and happiness, though both died as losers of their respective contests—the latter, of course, becoming the exemplar par excellence of the *perfectus Stoicus,* or ideal Stoic wise man in Roman culture?[48]

Recovering alcoholics and addicts universally speak of living new emotional lives. The original "solution" to their emotional disturbance, whether low spirits or high, has been removed from their lives. Without the bottle of whiskey or pills to turn off emotional experience, the recovering individual must work on the development of a new set of emotional tools. In the next chapter, I will analyze in depth a variety of these tools, but for now I want to focus on how Stoic *apatheia* with its lessons in detachment and the stochastic approach to one's aims offers valuable insight into the serenity and peace of mind that Twelve-Step recovery holds out as the emotional goal above all others.

Let us take a far from uncommon experience in the life of the recovering individual and examine it in Stoic terms. It is well recognized by psychiatrists, psychologists, and recovery counselors that alcoholism is a "family disease." Not only are fathers and daughters and brothers and sisters much more likely to share the disease than two strangers, but the disease of family extends to friendships. Alcoholics tend quite unerringly to find friends who drink like they do. For the recovering individual this creates a situation where they will more than likely have a family member or friend who is sober aiming to get them into AA, or they will be the sober one hoping for recovery for brother, lover, or friend. Passionate love of the person in question, while no doubt existing, is the enemy of both the recovering person and the still-using alcoholic. "Detach with love" is the first advice many an old-timer in AA will offer in such a scenario. Why? It is precisely because passionate feeling distorts the objective and rational recognition of the situation. By practicing Stoic *apatheia* the recovering person will not only better preserve their own serenity, so vital to their own continuing recovery, but also do the greatest good for the imperiled friend or family member. It is never recommended that friends or family members enter into sponsor/sponsee relationships for this same reason. The recognition of one's personal powerlessness to save their friend or family member is the wisdom of detachment. After all, for each person who has found lasting recovery, it was the same recognition of their powerlessness over their disease and the acceptance of their complete defeat that led to freedom and victory. A commonly heard phrase used by those describing their moments of clarity that led them to recovery is "surrender to win."

In aiming to point their family member, lover, or friend in the direction of recovery, the recovering person can benefit by adopting the Stoic stochastic approach as well. But it is perhaps most apt to the role of sponsor. Famously, no one can get another person sober. Each must do this for themself. However, sponsors are an extremely vital part of the process for most. A sponsor must have a detached stochastic perspective. To become overly invested in outcomes, successful recovery for their sponsee or its opposite (up to and including death) is to engage passionately with a goal over which they have no ultimate power, a guaranteed path to frustration and misery. One does what one can to aid with the training of the newly sober individual, but if they return to drinking and are lost to the disease, this is by no means to be defined as a failure. The training the sponsor engages in is the aiming; and so long as they are still sober and recovering, the victory over alcoholism in their own lives remains steadfast in spite of the victory of alcoholism over the sponsee.[49] Bill Wilson found that for him the strongest medicine against picking up a drink was in trying to help another alcoholic, not necessarily being successful in his attempt.

Figure 1. Illustration of Epictetus in Edward Ivie's 1715 Latin translation of Enchiridion. Credit: Image scanned by the John Adams Library at the Boston Public Library, Public Domain.

2

The *Armamentarium* of Epictetus and Marcus Aurelius

The Stoic Treasury of Psychological Weaponry and the AA "Toolbox"

The emotional compass of early recovery finds its true north in serenity. In the first chapter we saw how one vision of this kind of serenity might be conceived in the *apatheia* of the Stoics. While keeping truth north in mind, it is safe to say that recovery most often takes a meandering course. Along the course of our journey navigating an emotional map that we had blotted out through our drinking, a new way of handling emotions becomes a central focus. The ancient philosophical school that offers the most well-developed and systematically integrated techniques of emotion regulation is that whose very name, through the victory of its philosophical critics in the etymological evolution of the English language, has rather ironically come not to be associated with the regulation of emotion, but rather with the wholesale elimination or extirpation of the emotions. In English popular usage, "stoical" has devolved into a description of one "showing austere indifference to joy, grief, pleasure, or pain."[1] But in sharp contrast to this common understanding, the Stoics in fact focused a great deal of their philosophical acumen and rigor on emotion regulation in their aim to experience a sense of flowing joy.

Once the training and habituation in the fundamental Stoic perspectives discussed in Chapter 1 have been established, it is time to turn to the acquisition and honing of specific techniques from Stoic moral psychology directed to emotion regulation in much the same way recovering addicts emphasize the development of tools for handling situations where they formerly turned to their favored substance for escape. At the close of the first chapter, we looked at how the Stoics and Epictetus, specifically, advocated for the development of a detached, process-oriented approach to our aims in life that corresponds quite closely with the AA perspective on releasing control of outcomes. The stochastic approach focuses on intention and process rather than on outcomes. This highly valuable technique is, in fact, but one of several "weapons" Epictetus suggests we learn to wield to wrangle the ever so dangerous beasts of human emotional experience. AAs likewise talk frequently of either a "set of tools" or "the AA toolbelt," which they have picked up and learned to utilize over the course of recovery to handle the frustration, resentment, sadness, confusion, giddiness, joy, contentment, and so forth of "life on life's terms."

When one thinks of where to turn for help with regulating their emotional experience, the first answer likely to come to mind in a modern context is psychotherapy of one variety or another. Indeed, a good number of people in recovery do seek and find help beyond the AA program from counselors, therapists, psychologists, and psychiatrists. What additional advantage can be found in turning to the Stoics, then? Strikingly, the Stoics lie at the very root of the techniques found to be most effective in the regulation of emotions in the most wide-ranging research studies psychologists have conducted in recent years. These studies affirm that the techniques of Cognitive Behavioral Therapy (CBT) are the most effective of the various schools of psychotherapy.[2] And the Stoics are the ancestors of CBT as its founders, Albert Ellis (1913–2007) and Aaron Beck (1921–2021), both confirm in their own writings. As Epictetus guided us through the Stoic *askesis* of recovery in Chapter 1 through the analogy of combat training, so here he will lead us into the realm of modern psychology through the analysis of the foundational relationship between CBT and its techniques and his philosophical thinking and its applicability to the recovering person's journey in sobriety.

Cognitive Distancing and Objective Representation

One of the most effective techniques in emotion regulation is that known as Cognitive Distancing in Cognitive Behavioral Therapy. Beck defines it as follows: "'Distancing' refers to the ability to view one's own thoughts (or beliefs) as constructions of 'reality' rather than as reality itself." The psychological instruction here is matched by the Stoic practice of *phantasia kataleptike*, or "objective representation" in Hadot's translation.[3] Both Epictetus and Marcus Aurelius make frequent reference to the practice. One example should suffice here. In a discourse on how to handle *phantasiai* or impressions that come upon one in life, the kinds of impressions that might evoke a strong emotional response, Epictetus enjoins his students to handle these impressions by never giving assent to anything other than a *phantasia kataleptike*:

> His son died. Nothing other than this? Not one thing. The ship was lost. What has happened? The ship was lost. He was led away to jail. What happened? He was led away to jail. The idea that "He has fared badly" is something which each man *adds*[4] from himself.
>
> (*Discourses* 3.8.5)

The repetition of the objective verbal statement of the facts of the situation without the addition of a value judgment found here in Epictetus' advice to his students is identical to the basis of Ellis's ABC, "activation-belief-consequence" model, an early formulation of his Rational Emotive Behavioral Therapy, the precursor to the wider field of CBT. Ellis gives credit to Epictetus and the Stoics in numerous places in describing the origin of his cognitive approaches.[5] Ellis, like Epictetus before him, saw that the creation of objective distance at the belief or assent stage where value judgments are added was the key to regulating emotional response. If one can suspend value judgments through objective representation, then one can regulate emotion through correcting erroneous value judgments at the belief stage. It is here we add the value judgments that lead directly to negative emotions. As Sorabji notes, "Stoicism trains you to stand back from appearances and interrogate them without automatically giving them the assent of your reason."[6]

While Epictetus' examples are extreme in nature as they involve the death of a child, the sinking of a ship, and imprisonment, we ought not allow the examples used to obscure the central point that it is in the addition of a value judgment where the problem lies. Here is the source of emotional disturbance—or at least the majority of it, according to the Stoics and practitioners of CBT. Perhaps Marcus Aurelius' gentler examples will help here:

> "The gherkin[7] is bitter." Put it down. "Briars are on the roadway." Change direction. This is sufficient. Don't say in *addition*: "How can things like this happen in the universe?!" Since you would be mocked by anyone with a true understanding of nature.

Epictetus would challenge us in terms of the big, emotional disturbances of life we might handle at an advanced stage of philosophical progress. Marcus brings us to more mundane irritations. AAs certainly frequently encounter both and need to learn to utilize tools for dealing with both.

Let us consider the alcoholic's emotional handling of situations more in the Aurelian vein, for now. I personally knew an alcoholic who would utilize any delay in the metro train service of his major city on a given day as a justification for heading directly to a bar. In thousands of meetings over the years, I have heard similarly ridiculous (to the nonalcoholic, all too relatable to the alcoholic) reactions to things for which, as Marcus would put it, the knowing person would mock us. Nonalcoholics also experience outsize emotional outbursts to the briars on the roadway in the form of modern traffic snarls, as the phenomenon of "road rage" has shown us all repeatedly. To the Stoic and CBT practitioner the error in our mounting anger and frustration at such things resides in a phase between the event and our reaction to it. It is the addition of a value judgment to our experience. Instead of "there is a massive traffic backup" leading to "this is horrible because it will make me late" and even worse, "this is so unfair; I'm being persecuted by the universe," the Stoic suggests training in avoiding the "this is horrible" statement. Instead, one might take the more objective view of a traffic reporter and say to oneself, "Well, this is to be expected at this time of day on this road," or "Accidents are inevitable and merely a matter of probability, another name for reality."

As was touched upon in Chapter 1, the alcoholic has less-developed skills for dealing with frustration than others because they have spent some meaningful portion of their lives coping by means of a substance rather than cultivating emotional agility. It is thus vitally important that the recovering person learn to accept reality and avoid escapism. Objective representation is one of the most fundamental and effective means of doing so. As many in AA will be quick to assert, acceptance is a critical tool of recovery for regulation of one's emotional experience. In fact, it is fair to say that the most well-known section of the "Big Book" of Alcoholics Anonymous not written by Bill Wilson is a passage from the story of a physician who eloquently speaks to the central position of acceptance in his program of recovery:

> And acceptance is the answer to *all* my problems today. When I am disturbed, it is because I find some person, place, thing, or situation—some fact of my life—unacceptable to me, and I can find no serenity until I accept that person, place, thing, or situation as being exactly the way it is supposed to be at this moment.
>
> (*Alcoholics Anonymous*, 4th ed., 417)

Both the Stoic and the cognitive behavioral therapist would here emphasize that there is a point in our reaction to many facts of life at which we have the tendency to proclaim, "This is unacceptable!" Once spoken, we have rendered the fact unacceptable to ourselves and only frustration, resentment, anger, and unhappiness can follow.

For alcoholics in recovery, the first value judgment to avoid is about the fact of having the disease of alcoholism. AA has been particularly useful in this regard, as the disease model of alcoholism, outlined in the "Big Book" in the "The Doctor's Opinion" preface, reveals to many an alcoholic for the first time that their disease is not a moral failing or evidence of weak character. Unfortunately, many alcoholics still get stuck on the equation, "I'm a drunk" = "I'm a *bad* person," a highly destructive addition of a judgment to the fact of their disease. Psychotherapists working in addiction focus on self-compassionate acceptance as critical for the addict. Marlatt, Bowen, and Lustyk, for example, "have incorporated the critical elements of wisdom and compassion to help people with addictive behaviors learn to avoid the trap of seeing their behavior as 'bad' and blaming themselves—judgments that motivate substance abuse."[8] Here we are entering territory that forms a bridge from objective representation to the next

Stoic psychological technique to be investigated, the nonjudgmental viewing of one's own thoughts and feelings.

Stoic *Propatheiai* "Proto-Passions" and Nonjudgmental Self-Evaluation in CBT

The three psychotherapists quoted above at the close of the first section advocate a program called MBRP (Mindfulness-Based Relapse Prevention). It is itself modeled on an ancient philosophical tradition: *vipassana,* or insight practice in Buddhism. Not surprisingly, it shares a great deal with the practices Epictetus advocates for meditative self-evaluation. I say not surprisingly here because the Stoics are often linked to Buddhists in philosophical perspective and practice. In fact, Epictetus has acquired among some scholars and lovers of philosophy the nickname "Roman Buddha" through the years. The psychotherapists describe the process and benefits of MBRP as follows:

> The practices and discussion throughout the course focus on two basic questions: What is actually happening? What does my mind do with what is happening? By learning to differentiate between what arises (e.g., a physical sensation or an emotion) from how we relate to it (e.g., with judgment, aversion, clinging), we develop flexibility—whatever arises, we have a choice in how we respond. This is where we find freedom.[9]

Within the Stoic system there is an identical technique, one that separates involuntary emotional reactions known in Stoic terms as *propatheiai* (proto-passions) from the truly dangerous emotions, the passions based on erroneous beliefs to which one has given one's assent. In recovery terms, the *propatheiai* correspond to reactive emotional states rather than responsive ones at the arrival of an emotionally charged bit of news.

A famous Stoic anecdote about the relationship between these proto-passions and the true passions, and the Stoic's suspension of judgment that stops the first from becoming the second, is found in Aulus Gellius (*c.* 125 CE–180 CE). In his *Attic Nights*, a collection of wisdom from the worlds of history, philosophy, geography, science, and more, he relates the tale of a Stoic philosopher with whom he was sailing when a severe storm threatened destruction of the ship and her company.[10] Gellius observes that the Stoic philosopher does not engage in any of the hysterical behavior of the other passengers, yet he is very clearly affected by the danger posed by the storm. His face turns white, his hands shake, and he appears generally disturbed. After the storm passes, Gellius inquires of the philosopher about his response to the storm, wondering whether his Stoic beliefs ought not to have prevented him from having any kind of fearful reaction at all. The philosopher then produces a volume of Epictetus from his bag and allows Gellius to read Epictetus' explanation of the proto-passions in relation to the true passions. A brief excerpt illuminates the point here:

> That is why, when some terrifying sound occurs, either from the sky or from the collapse of a building or as the sudden herald of some danger, even the wise person's mind necessarily responds and is contracted and grows pale for a little while, not because

> he opines that something evil is at hand, but by certain rapid and unplanned movements antecedent to the office of intellect and reason. Shortly, however, the wise person in that situation "witholds assent" from those terrifying mental impressions, he spurns and rejects them and does not think that there is anything in them which he should fear.[11]

The value of this Stoic perspective to emotional sobriety, the daily and continuous central goal of true recovery, is clear. It might be less obvious what use a person early in recovery and still suffering from the wracking craving of the body for and obsession of the mind with their removed substance can make of such regulation of one's psyche. But craving is, in fact, a proto-passion on a neurochemical level, an inescapable physiological and psychological reaction of the addict. It turns out that "withholding assent" can be a lifesaver when experiencing such symptoms. Intense craving feelings typically last between ten and twenty minutes. Recognizing one's cravings as an unavoidable proto-passion, but one that will subside in a short period of time, provides a useful perspective on handling the intensity of craving in the early stages of recovery.[12]

The in-the-moment strategy of suspension of judgment is a useful technique. However, as the empirical data show, it is really the combining of strategies for emotion regulation that leads to the best results of all.[13] In the terms of AA's most common metaphor of the emotional toolbox, this explains why having both a wrench and a hammer in your toolbox is better than having just a wrench. Cognitive strategies with mixed reappraisal techniques—e.g., objective representation with suspension of judgment to combine the first two techniques discussed above—displayed the greatest overall effectiveness in the meta-analysis of professional psychology researchers. I wish to propose here a Stoic explanation for why the empirical data show that a combination of reappraisal techniques matching Stoic practices proves to be far and away the most effective set of tools for emotion regulation by taking a closer look at the synergistic and self-reinforcing nature of the Stoic *armamentarium*, or treasury of psychological weaponry, utilized by a Stoic in regulating their emotional life.

The greatest defense against the danger of proto-passions (*propatheiai*) becoming passions (*pathei*), the sources of emotional disturbance via the carrying away of one's rational perspective, is in forming a constant habit of reappraisal that cuts the wire on the circuit leading from proto-passion to passion. As Davidson summarizes it, "The askesis of the Stoics is nothing but the process of generating stronger internal compulsion."[14] It is this stronger internal compulsion routinized via habit that counteracts *propatheiai*. Progressing from in-the-moment techniques, the Stoic *askesis* aims at regulation of those things that regulate emotion: our desires and fears. Our desires can be tempered and redirected through the Stoic *askesis*. Through practice, which leads to a deeper and deeper cognitive absorption of the suspension of assent and the suspension of value judgments through objective representation, the Stoic moves toward a more fundamental change in their beliefs about the very nature of good and bad. It is here that training grounded in moral psychology transitions to an entire ethic of life. Through the generation of a stronger internal compulsion that redirects our desires, we open room for the more fundamental changes in belief about the nature of our desires.

One of AA's most frequently heard and most succinct sayings on how the program changes lives, "I came for my drinking, but stayed for my thinking," reflects the same essential change the Stoics are advocating. Stoics move from a psychological strategy for a specific desire to a whole new way of seeing desire itself and its role in their lives differently. Recovering folks must do the same to move from physical sobriety to psychical sobriety, which brings the promises of the program with it.

In the next section we will examine the Stoic strategy of delimitation of the present, not as a stand-alone technique but in combination with objective representation and suspension of judgment. The aim here will be to see how the Stoic *askesis* of Chapter 1 can bring these techniques into a systematized way of life, a habit of being, or *hexis* in the Stoic terminology. As the Stoic-in-training learns to employ the *praecepta,* or ethical injunctions, as exercises continuously in their life through *askesis*, these *praecepta* dovetail with and are underpinned more permanently by the *decreta*, or actual philosophical doctrines.

Delimitation of the Present in Stoicism and Living One Day at a Time in AA

Even those only acquainted with AA through representations from movies and television are likely to be familiar with the ubiquity of the "it's a one day at a time" program mantra of its members. It is so often repeated in the program because it is so central to living life in recovery. The alcoholic's impulsive reaction, deeply ingrained by both neurochemistry and habit, to regrets and sadness about the past and fears and anxieties about the future is to reach for the bottle. The recovering person must endeavor to get better and better at living in the present to remain sober and progress spiritually. Here the Stoics can offer philosophical reasoning and perspective to reinforce the injunction to become more centered in the present.

Marcus Aurelius (121 CE–180 CE), Epictetus' spiritual successor, provides a particularly lucid example of how this process works through his continual repetition of *praecepta* concerning the Stoic focus on the present as the only reality and the only time in which *eudaimonia* or happiness can be realized:

> Thence remind yourself that it is not the future nor the past which weighs on you, but always the present, but this time is made small, if you circumscribe it to itself and you cross-examine and convict your mind if it is not able to endure this tiny bit of time.
>
> (*Meditations* VIII.36)

The repetition of meditations on bringing one's attention to the present moment, a mindfulness known to the Stoics as *prosoche*, is useful in its own right for regulating one's emotional experience. But Marcus wishes us to grasp that the *askesis*, the meditations or exercises themselves, are supported fundamentally by an understanding of Stoic doctrines about both time and value. The French philosopher Pierre Hadot (1922–2010), one of the most influential modern philosophers in his embrace of the Stoics for their training in living, draws the connection specifically between exhortations about staying in the present and the wider Stoic program of elimination of value judgments:

> This process of delimiting the present is entirely analogous to the process by means of which we hold fast to the facts and to reality in our objective and adequate representations, and refuse to add

> value-judgements to them. There is, after all, a sense in which the value-judgements which trouble us are always related either to the past or to the future.[15]

In other words, objective representation and delimitation of the present arise from the same reasoned truth about ontology: the past, the future, and value judgments are all untruths in that they are not grounded in reality; they don't exist![16] Marcus in another meditation emphasizes how much focus on the present aids one in keeping representation of *phantasiai* ("appearances") objective.[17] The synergy and shared origin of the Stoic practices are here very clearly revealed. A firm grasp of Stoic philosophical doctrine about the nature of the present as the only time that belongs to us or is up to us, in the language of the fundamental Epictetan dichotomy from Chapter 1, reinforces the practice of objective representation. To Marcus, then, Stoicism operates as the reinforcing of precepts utilized in daily exercises by the doctrine that gives them meaning within an entire system of life. In other words, the psychological technique now has a Stoic philosophical grounding.

The Stoic perspective echoes and clarifies the recovery principle of "just for today." Consider just how closely the following Hazelden meditation matches Marcus' words on the weight of the past and future discussed above:

> You are so made that you can only carry the weight of twenty-four hours, no more. If you weigh yourself down with the years behind and the days ahead, your back breaks. God has promised to help with the burdens of the day only. If you are foolish enough to gather again that burden of the past and carry it, then indeed you cannot

expect God to help you bear it. So forget that which lies behind you and breathe in the blessing of each new day. (*Twenty-Four Hours a Day*—January 2nd Meditation for the Day)

Experienced AAs remind newcomers to take it one day at a time precisely because the idea of weeks, months, and years in sobriety can weigh quite heavily on their shoulders just as Marcus speaks of the weight of time not our own in the meditation discussed above. At the other end of the recovery spectrum, not a few old-timers with fifteen, twenty, or thirty years of continuous sobriety insist on adding the phrase "one day at a time" whenever they declare their number of years clean as a reminder they did not get to such an expanse of clean time in any other fashion than by striving to live in the present. Those progressing in sobriety often find that delimiting the present helps to reduce the regret and guilt associated with the years lost to the bottle. Delimiting the present mitigates for newcomers an often crippling anxiety about upcoming legal, financial, and relationship woes brought on by drinking that brought them to the rooms of AA. Anxiety about the future leads us naturally to the next Stoic technique to integrate into our lives and programs, namely the premeditation of misfortunes.

Praemeditatio Malorum and "A Design for Living That Works in Rough Going"

The Stoic practice of *praemeditatio malorum*, the contemplation of misfortunes in advance, is specifically formulated to address our difficulties as human beings in delimiting the present. This is just one example of the way in which Stoicism is strikingly pragmatic in accepting our likelihood of merely intermittent success in the deployment of the psychological *armamentarium*. Our thoughts tend to drift into the future and then dwell there for extended periods. The result is worry, the by-product of attempting to control the uncontrollable by finding solutions for problems that aren't even yet present. The Stoic countertechnique asserts our agency in the present in a powerful, if somewhat counterintuitive, manner. This practice asks us to imagine—in as much concrete, objective detail as possible—the worst possible outcome to those situations in the future that cause us worry. Worry feeds on what psychologists term "intolerance of uncertainty." *Praemeditatio,* on the other hand, asks us to accept the worst outcomes as possibilities and realize that even if they should come to pass, we will be fine if we can practice acceptance of what and what is not up to us. In realizing this, we "decatastrophize" the possible outcomes that cause us such anxiety as well as allow ourselves head space for eliminating surprises and rehearsing coping mechanisms.[18] Rather than being victimized as passive spectators of our own worried minds, with *praemediatio* we take back agency in the present over the future by accepting its inherently uncontrollable nature.

Praemeditatio malorum may well prove most useful to the recovering individual in their setting of goals. Many newly sober individuals strive to make up for time and energy lost to addiction by setting out to accomplish goals they perhaps abandoned years earlier because alcohol had taken over their lives. The setting of goals is a positive and worthwhile habit to form in recovery, especially for those who lost all sight of what they wanted out of life in the depths of their disease. But here the recovery mantra "Easy Does It" is particularly applicable. The meeting rooms of AA are filled with people returning from relapse who tell the same story: I got sober; I felt better; I set forth to accomplish those things alcohol had stood in the way of; I achieved those things and I put recovery on the back burner to my new life, and here I am again having lost my sobriety and all those things. A memorable formulation for this in the rooms occurs in the saying, "Whatever you put before your sobriety will be the second thing you lose." The Stoic practice of premeditation can help us keep our goals in perspective.

Let us take thought of common goals, the attendant emotional experience associated with them, and a Stoic insight on the nature of goals that premeditation can aid us in understanding. The most severe anxiety about the future tends to center around those goals we hold dearest. Whatever these goals look like, be they the purchase of a new home, a promotion at work, the completion of a large-scale undertaking, the starting of family, and myriad other possible worthy projects, we as humans tend to focus on accomplishment, achievement, and outcome. The Stoic sees a great flaw in such thinking. Take the job promotion as an example. For the last five years a person has excelled at their job, accruing awards for contributions to the company, gaining the recognition and respect of colleagues and higher-ups alike. A promotion from a junior-level position to something more senior had been on the table, with 2020 as the year within the internal promotion structure in which this would likely take place. But the pandemic arrived, shook up company financial considerations, and the promotion was taken off the table, perhaps never to resurface as a possibility. Default human reactions to this event might involve resentment, depression, lack of motivation, and more.

For the alcoholic, such a situation is even more serious. Bill Wilson emphasizes repeatedly in the "Big Book" that resentment, beyond all other emotional experiences, is the most dangerous threat there is to sobriety. His most well-known statement to this effect is downright harrowing: "Resentment is the number one offender. It destroys more alcoholics than anything else. From it stem all forms of spiritual disease."[19] Resentment is an emotional experience that alcoholics typically "drink at." In other words, it is a spur to the progression of the disease. We need look no further than English word usage to see this for ourselves. Think of the verb "to stew." When one stews in a negative emotion, it only intensifies that emotion. For the alcoholic, this leads to more and more drinking, to getting "stewed." Where a nonalcoholic might get down about the loss of the promotion possibility in the example above, the alcoholic is likely to turn over a table at the company Christmas party when their resentment boils over and get fired as a result.

The Stoic locates the problem in the thinking surrounding the potential promotion in the first place, rather than in the aftermath. This is because the outcome, something not up to the individual, became the focus, rather than the process, which is entirely up to the individual. Cicero (106 BCE–43 BCE) has Cato the Younger (95 BCE–46 BCE), the man recognized by the Romans as the fullest incarnation of the Stoic sage, explain the Stoic perspective via a metaphor from archery in his *De Finibus Bonorum et Malorum*, "On the Ends of Good and Evil":

> If a man were to make it his purpose to take a true aim with a spear or arrow at some mark, his ultimate end, corresponding to the

> ultimate good as we pronounce it, would be to do all he could to aim straight: the man in this illustration would have to do everything to aim straight, yet, although he did everything to attain his purpose, his "ultimate End," so to speak, would be what corresponded to what we call the Chief Good in the conduct of life, whereas the actual hitting of the mark would be in our phrase "to be chosen" but not "to be desired."
>
> (*De Fin.* III.22)

Our goal should be thought of as target, or *skopos,* in Greek. We, as archers, can take care of our bow and arrows to make sure they are in the best condition, train rigorously to become the best possible shot we can, perfect our footwork, control our breathing, and focus our thoughts, but when the given day comes for the archery contest, it is entirely possible that something may not go our way. A gust of wind, a slip of a foot, a sneeze from a spectator, any of these could take our arrow off target and result in the "failed outcome" of not hitting the mark. Here Cato explains that we ought to distinguish the target, the hitting of which involves factors outside of us, from the true goal or *telos* of exercising our agency, virtue, and wisdom. The employee having contributed to their company, earned recognition and respect, and developed their skill set has accomplished a much more central goal than the promotion, which in Stoic terms was simply a target and not the real goal. The employee has grown as an agent of rational and virtuous action. Stoicism asks us to focus more on these internal goals, which are part of the process of aiming at external targets as the more lasting and meaningful accomplishments in our lives. To obtain the promotion is what is known as a "preferred indifferent" in Stoicism, or what Cato above calls something "to be chosen" but not "to be desired." Success at the art of life resides in the act of aiming well. Becoming something, a good archer or a valuable employee: these are virtuous goals. Hitting targets and getting promotions: these may or may not occur due to many other variables. Process trumps outcome every time. This is a further conceptualization of the stochastic nature of the life of Stoic virtue discussed in terms of winning and losing versus improving as an athlete discussed at the close of Chapter 1.

In AA, the emotional disturbances stemming from missed targets in the recovering person's life are often mitigated by the maintenance of the larger life of virtue in much the same way. After all, maintaining physical sobriety while continuously developing one's emotional sobriety are the real goals beyond all external attainments. Premeditation can aid us in broadening our perspective on what are targets as opposed to real goals in the life of recovery. Contemplating the possibility of the missed job promotion lessens anxiety if things do, in fact, turn out that way. Even more importantly, it serves to remind the recovering person that an individual target may not be achieved, but a life of emotional sobriety allows for the handling of all sorts of disappointments and crises. The focus shifts from what one aims to achieve to who one wants to become. *The Grapevine*, a monthly magazine for those in AA, published a daily quote book in 2012. The entry for April 15 reads as if written by a recovering alcoholic listening to a modern Cato's advice: "My sponsor … gave me some advice. 'Take the words *success* and *failure* out of your vocabulary. Replace them with *honesty* and *effort*.'"[20]

The Stoic *armamentarium* is a philosophically reasoned and argued version of one part of what AAs call "the toolbox" or "toolbelt." These expressions denote the emotional terms learned from practice of the Twelve Steps, reading of AA literature, meeting attendance, service to the program and other alcoholics, conversation with friends and advisors, and more. But they also point to certain philosophical perspectives deriving from these sources that include strategies for the handling of emotional distress, staying in the present, and being prepared for the adversity life will assuredly send their way.

Figure 2. The Dying Seneca by Peter Paul Rubens (1577–1640). Credit: Alte Pinakothek in Munich, Germany, Public Domain.

3

Tranquility in the Midst of Tempest

Seneca and a Living Metaphor for the Serenity of Recovery

Having first allowed Epictetus to guide us through the Stoic approach to habit formation in the cultivation of a sober practice of life, and then examined the Stoic toolbox equipped by both Epictetus and Marcus Aurelius for the handling of our emotions, it is time we turn to another Roman Stoic for insight on that which may at times feel the most elusive goal but also the most profoundly meaningful reward of the sober life, namely the serenity that arises out of emotional sobriety. The centrality and ubiquity of the "Serenity Prayer" within the program is clear evidence of this. It is routinely used as the opening to an AA meeting and often as the closing as well. It is far and away the prayer people speak of most often in their shares as a mantra they turn to for getting through a wide variety of challenging life circumstances. And "serenity" is one of the most, if not the most, frequently used words in the names individual AA meeting groups give themselves, e.g., Serenity at Sunrise or Sundown or at the Beach or on the Mountain.[1] Here is the prayer, previously discussed in relation to Epictetus' dichotomy of control, back in Chapter 1:

> God, grant me the serenity to accept the things I cannot
> change, the courage to change the things I can,
> and the wisdom to know the difference.

Why are the word "serenity" and the prayer so powerful for alcoholics? More than any other single word, the word "serenity" conjures up the achievement of emotional sobriety and therefore encapsulates all that is the antithesis of the drinking life with its constant chaotic upheavals and the stress born of these that only escape into a drink could quell—until, of course, it couldn't. To live "life on life's terms," as one of AA's most common phrases goes, and to feel serene while doing so, is considered the daily goal of living a truly recovering life.

Seneca (4 BCE–65 CE) also viewed serenity as a central goal of the philosophical life. His term for it in Latin is *tranquillitas* (our English word "tranquility"), a word he chooses specifically for its metaphorical richness. But before we dig into Seneca, we must first ask what role metaphor plays in recovery. The sober alcoholic most often meets with metaphors for the kinds of changes recovery requires in meditation literature. Most alcoholics formulate for themselves some kind of daily meditation practice; many turn to a wide variety of inspirational daily readers to provide a quote related to their journey of recovery that may serve as an impetus to contemplation. Holding a recovery-centered thought or two or three in their mind from the beginning of the day helps the alcoholic to remember the disease that lies dormant within them and take positive action in the direction of mitigating many of the other "-isms" that coalesce around alcoholism. A reminder to stay in the day, for example, helps fight off what many alcoholics describe as their default mental state of living in regret about the past and fear about the future. Some of these daily meditation books are published by AA itself and utilized as sources for subject matter for participants in meetings to reflect and comment upon (*Daily Reflections, As Bill Sees It, The Grapevine Daily Quote Book*). Some are published by recovery-centered organizations outside of AA, like the Hazelden Betty Ford Foundation.

The Hazelden series is a particularly popular one for at-home meditation practice, so it seems a reasonable place from which to draw an example. The entry in their *Touchstones* book for August 3 is this quote from Henri J. M. Nouwen, followed by a couple of paragraphs of reflection:

> To live a spiritual life we must first find the courage to enter into the desert of loneliness and to change it by gentle and persistent efforts into a garden of solitude.[2]

What is intriguing here is the ethical work that the metaphor performs. Through the contemplation of the metaphor, we are asked not simply to learn how being alone may be a positive experience rather than a negative one for the spiritual seeker and liver, but further that negative aloneness, loneliness, is marked by the absence of cultivation through the author's use of the desert imagery. "Desert" literally means a place where no seed can be sown, so as a metaphor it richly evokes the feelings of uselessness, worthlessness, and helplessness that often accompany loneliness. Conversely, positive aloneness, solitude, is a place of cultivation and growth through the garden imagery.

Taoism, a philosophy whose proximity to Stoicism allows for very illuminating comparisons (as shall be discussed extensively in the next chapter), can help enrich our understanding of how the Stoics employ a metaphor. Taoism makes very rich use of metaphors for shaping one's own psychological perspective and following a truly thought-out ethical life. Consider the following, found in a Taoist meditation on spirituality and metaphysics:

> Metaphor is essentially a way to shape thoughts. The insights of poetry can often guide us out of problems; the imagery of an opening flower is often used in meditation.[3]

The shaping of one's thoughts for the day is the core purpose of a morning meditation practice in recovery so we can see that metaphor and poetry are intricately tied together in a recovering life.

More than any other Stoic, Greek or Roman, Seneca preferred to operate in the same manner as the Hazelden and Taoist meditations above. He worked through his philosophical ideas in metaphor and imagery. Unlike Epictetus, whose ideas are presented as they were delivered to his classes in an aphoristic lecturing style of Greek, Seneca wished to use his native language of Latin for its imagistic power to *paint* his philosophy. This has the effect of sometimes making him difficult to turn to for straightforward ethical advice, but in turn renders his Stoicism particularly apt for the deeper contemplation of core concepts like serenity.

In his *De Tranquillitate Animi* ("On Serenity of Mind"), Seneca's metaphorical method is especially notable because of the way in which his own choice of philosophical vocabulary for the state of Stoic peace of mind, *tranquillitas*, acts as both source and point of return for a ship of soul metaphor through which he elucidates the tenets of his moral psychology. Seneca produces a detailed portrait of the Stoic way of life that leads to serenity by getting his reader to really see in their mind's eye their soul as a ship on the sea sailing through tranquil waters. The full portrait of the ethical goal of the treatise is produced through the interaction of the Greek Stoic concept of *euthymia* ("harmonious spirit") with *tranquillitas*, the Latin term Seneca selects for the Greek concept, and the metaphor inherent within it that is developed as a dominant theme throughout the text. The process is exemplary of what Brad Inwood, a leading scholar on Seneca, characterizes by saying that Seneca "prefers to work his ideas out in Latin, in Latin terms, because that is the language he thinks in."[4] The net effect of Seneca's working out of the term *tranquillitas* through the ship of soul metaphor is a Stoic moral psychological *telos*, or goal, that encompasses heterodox philosophical elements, principally from Epicureanism, and a fundamentally Roman *ethos* while retaining its core Stoic nature.

This chapter will lead us through a deep contemplation of Stoic serenity in the terms of Seneca's ship of soul metaphor through a close reading. In other words, this chapter should serve as a kind of portrait for extended meditation on the kind of psychological serenity the recovering person seeks to attain.

In the first section I will analyze Seneca's construction of the moral psychology of the term *tranquillitas* in relation to both Greek Stoic and native Roman concepts. Furthermore, this section will examine how the personal psychological struggle of Seneca's pupil Serenus both anticipates and develops the ship of soul metaphor. Serenus will serve as a proxy for the recovering individual making progress toward emotional sobriety and Seneca as a proxy for his sponsor.

In the next part I will focus on how Stoic strategies for emotion regulation—some discussed in Chapter 2 and some first introduced here, including premeditation of misfortune, the reserve clause, and emulation of the sage—are powerfully invoked through the specific language of the metaphor of the ship of soul. We will see how Seneca paints the psychological tools into his picture of serenity.

In the third and final part I will consider what it means to think through a philosophical concept in metaphorical terms by considering the rich philosophical potential of metaphor in Seneca's usage. In succinctly conveying multiple philosophical concepts in one term where Marcus Aurelius utilizes three in his own employment of the ship of soul metaphor, Seneca brings coherence to the Stoic worldview, which allows for the seeming paradox of experiencing serenity in the midst of psychological turmoil. I will examine what is unique about Seneca's employment of metaphor and both contextualize and analyze it in terms of common uses of metaphor and a richer engagement with metaphor as part of a process of developing philosophical content.

Picturing the Serenity of Recovery through the Roman Stoic Conception of *Tranquillitas*

Seneca explicates for his reader his choice of the term *tranquillitas* as the most apt translation of the concept the Greek Stoics call *euthymia*, a word that literally means "being in a good spiritual condition":

> Hanc stabilem animi sedem Graeci euthymian vocant, de qua Democriti volumen egregium est; ego tranquillitatem voco.
>
> The Greeks call this stable state of mind *euthymia*, concerning which the volume of Democritus is notable; I call this tranquility.
>
> (*De Tranq*. 2.3)

Seneca's choice of terminology has various implications, but those that point forward to the ship of soul metaphor are central. He selects a nonisomorphic (i.e., it is not made to match the Greek term one-for-one) term that is inherently imagistic and metaphorical in nature, since the early uses of the word in Latin often denote calmness of sea and/or wind.[5] But the reader need not be interested in seeking out the etymological history of *tranquillitas* to get what Seneca is after, since immediately prior to choosing the word both Serenus, his anxious pupil, and Seneca himself paint vivid portraits of the waveless calm he has in mind. Seneca makes his Serenus character define his mental disturbance in a way that anticipates Seneca's choice of term for Stoic *euthymia*:

> Rogo itaque, si quod habes remedium, quo hanc fluctationem meam sistas, dignum putes qui tibi tranquillitatem debeam.

> And thus it is that I ask, if you have any remedy by which you might stop this my state of fluctuation, if you think me a worthy kind of person to owe my tranquility to you.
>
> (*De Tranq.* 1.17)

Serenus describes his psychological struggle as a *fluctatio*, a side-to-side vacillation without cease, suggestive of the rocking of a ship by the waves. He requests Seneca provide the psychological tools to obtain *tranquillitas*—the significance of which term he doesn't yet fully understand. Seneca's choice of *tranquillitas* for *euthymia* is then anticipated prior to his explication of why he chooses the Latin psychological vocabulary he does. But Serenus' description of his *fluctatio* is the true form of anticipation of Seneca's metaphorical philosophizing:

> Non esse periculosos hos motus animi nec quicquam tumultuosi adferentis scio; ut vera tibi similitudine id, de quo queror, exprimam, non tempestate vexor sed nausea.
>
> I know that these movements of my mind are not dangerous nor the kind which bring real tumult; in order to explicate in a fitting metaphor that which I am complaining of, I am carried away not by a squall, but by seasickness.
>
> (*De Tranq.* 1.17)

Serenus' careful description of his psychological disturbance lays a clear foundation for the later metaphorical development of *tranquillitas* as the central *telos* of Seneca's construction of Stoic moral psychology. Serenus is importantly not overwhelmed in the *tempestas* "storm" of his psyche, but he is far from experiencing *tranquillitas*. *Fluctatio* is the unfortunate, but not critically dangerous, intermediate state of mind.[6] *Nausea* is the result of the *fluctatio* and carries the specific sense of seasickness here to suit the metaphorical picture.

Serenus' *fluctatio* is a picturesque way to contemplate the state of mind—described in the "Big Book" as feeling "restless, irritable, and discontent"[7]—common to recovering alcoholics on their less serene days. Alcoholics do not generally employ this phrase in reference to extreme stress or agitation of the kind that might lead to picking up a drink brought on by an intense shock like job loss, departure of a spouse, a bad accident, death of a loved one, or the like. Rather, "restless, irritable, and discontent" is a description of "the everyday malaise" that can result from skimping on one's spiritual program. Serenus' description of his state of mind as being not immediately dangerous but rather a form of psychological nausea is quite apt for painting a portrait of this negative but non-urgent state of mind. Another common AA phrase for this state is "being off the beam." This connotes a similar kind of wayward instability as Seneca's *fluctatio*.

By having Serenus give a clear picture of his state of mind as an intermediate between *tempestas* and *tranquillitas*, Seneca begins his treatise proper on the attainment of *tranquillitas* by not only building upon the inherent metaphorical imagery of the word *tranquillitas*, but more importantly by beginning to paint a picture of *tranquillitas* in terms of its opposition to both *tempestas* and *fluctatio*. Seneca poses the question to himself of how he ought to describe Serenus' state of mind "*cui talem adfectum animi similem putem*" ("to what should I say such a state of mind is similar?"; *De Tranq*. 2.1). He begins his answer with a description of the psychological condition by a working out through the metaphorical entailments of both Serenus' *fluctatio* and *nausea*, as well as an anticipatory nod to his own choice of *tranquillitas* as the subject of his treatise: *Sicut est quidam tremor etiam tranquilli maris, utique cum ex tempestate requievit* ("Just as there is still a tremor in a calm sea, as when it has just become calm after a storm"; *De Tranq.* 2.1). Worth consulting here is the very well-thought-out schema for how metaphors really "do work" in philosophical terms found in a lengthy footnote by Brad Inwood writing on Seneca:

> One might sketch out a typology of the relationships between metaphor and philosophical content. (1) The metaphor may be purely ornamental and evidently so, such that one feels no temptation to impute doctrinal significance to it; (2) at the other extreme, the metaphor may be an essential component of the philosopher's conception—his doctrine may have been developed by thinking through the metaphor itself and so the two are inextricably intertwined (the work of G. Lakoff and M. Johnson, *Metaphors We Live By* (Chicago, 1980) is interesting in this connection); (3) the metaphor may be used to enliven or reinforce the impact of a theory without being meant to determine the content of that theory, and in so doing it (i) may or (ii) may not introduce misleading elements or ideas; (4) there may be self-conscious analogies drawn to familiar experiences, analogies whose implications are meant to help determine the sense of a doctrine, and these analogies (i) may be essential to the justification of the theory or (ii) may be purely illustrative. There are surely many other possible categories.

In *De Tranquillitate* Seneca is fully engaged in the use of metaphor in sense (2). Through the invocation of the imagery of *tranquille mare* ("the tranquil sea"), Seneca points forward to his own chosen term for *euthymia* and reinforces Serenus' understanding that he is not in the thralls of a *tempestas*. But thus far the metaphorical imagery is primarily negative, a matter of emphasizing the more serious psychological disturbance that is *not* afflicting Serenus. After making his formal choice of *tranquillitas* for *euthymia*, however, Seneca begins to expand the metaphor in positive directions. In explaining how he seeks to convey not the *facies* (the formal appearance) but rather the *vis* (the force and meaning) of the Greek Stoic term, he stretches the metaphor of the calm sea in the direction of a favorable course or flow of water:

> Ergo quaerimus, quomodo animus semper aequali secundoque cursu eat propitiusque sibi sit et sua laetus aspiciat et hoc gaudium non interrumpat, sed placido statu maneat nec adtollens se umquam nec deprimens. Id tranquillitas erit.
>
> Therefore it is that we seek a way in which the mind may always proceed in a level and favorable course, be well-disposed to itself, and look on its own life situation with happiness and not break this joy, but rather remain in a peaceful condition by never either vaunting itself or depressing itself. This will be serenity.
>
> (*De Tranq.* 2.4)

Seneca here embraces within his definition of *tranquillitas* a wide array of concepts central to Stoic moral psychology, including *euroun* ("good flow") and *gaudium* ("joy"). The concept of *euroun* as a Stoic ideal invoked here by the phrase *aequali secundoque cursu* ("in a level and favorable course") goes back to Stoicism's founder, Zeno, and is central in Epictetan teaching as the ethical *telos* of *euroia biou* ("a good flow of life").[8] But this is merely one direction of the metaphorical valence of *tranquillitas.* As Smith convincingly shows, Seneca employs *tranquillitas* as "an amalgamation of different philosophical concepts—*apatheia* ("freedom from the passions"), *galena* ("gentle calm"), and *euthymia* ("being in a good spiritual condition")—but he is also "applying a traditional Roman term to *his* own conception of the ideal life."[9] What I focus on in the following section is how the ship of soul metaphor shapes Seneca's picture of the mind of a person living that ideal life.

Metaphor as Advice: General Guidelines for the Maintenance of Tranquility

In the first two chapters we examined a variety of specific Stoic psychological techniques for staying in the present, handling adversity, dealing with our emotions, and more. Now we shall take the picture of serenity Seneca paints for us and see how he applies his colors to the canvas to reveal how the Stoic techniques function within his metaphor.

The natural evocation of a calm sea, good flow, and smooth sailing in the use of *tranquillitas* allows Seneca to invoke the ethical *telos* while addressing specific strategies for obtaining it through development of the ship of soul metaphor. Of particular relevance to understanding

Seneca's use of the inherent metaphorical potential of *tranquillitas* is an early usage of the word by the Roman comic playwright Plautus (*c.* 254–184 BCE):

> Hic Favonius serenest, istic auster imbricus/Hic facit tranquillitatem, iste omnis fluctus conciet.
>
> "The Favonian Wind [i.e., the West Wind] is calm, from that side the Auster [i.e., the South Wind] wind brings rain/This one [the Favonian wind] makes for peaceful calm, that one [the south wind] will churn every wave."
>
> (Plautus, *Mercator* 877)[10]

Here the idea of serenity is for the first time in the history of Latin language expressed in terms of the tranquility of the sea. *Tranquillitas* also critically contains within its semantic range a distinct Roman flavor antecedent to its association with Greek philosophical vocabulary, as Cicero's usage of the term alongside *constantia* ("consistency") as hallmarks of *sanitas animi* ("good mental health") makes clear.[11] Seneca takes advantage of three specific valences of *tranquillitas*: firstly the evocative imagery of smooth sailing, secondly his choice of the word as the translation of the Greek *euthymia* ("being in a good spiritual condition"), and thirdly the psychological perspective on good mental health as defined by the *maiores* ("the Roman ancestors") in building the metaphor.

Beginning in section IX and proceeding through to section XIV of his treatise, Seneca utilizes the imagistic power of the ship of soul metaphor to highlight fundamental aspects of Stoic theory and practice.

> Cibus famem domet, potio sitim, libido qua necesse est fluat; discamus membris nostris inniti, cultum victumque non ad nova exempla componere, sed ut mairoum mores suadent.
>
> Let food tame hunger and drink thirst, let sexual desire flow where it is necessary; let us learn to rely on our own limbs and to arrange our clothing and lifestyle not to new examples, but in accordance with how the ways of our ancestors urge.
>
> (*De Tranq.* IX.2)

Here the choice of *fluat* ("let it flow") recalls the reader to the importance of flow in Stoic conceptions of serenity and points specifically to the smooth flow *of tranquillitas*, as Seneca's advice is to ward off *fluctus* ("fluctuation") or *tempestas* ("squall") brought on by unrestrained libido. The *mos maiorum* ("the ways of the ancestors") are then directly invoked immediately following to reflect the harmony between the traditional customs of sound Roman comportment and a calm flow of life contained within the term *tranquillitas*.

For the addict the ideas of flow and the craving born of an unhealthy desire are antithetical. The addict still actively using cannot "let it flow," as in let life take its natural course. Why not? Addiction is fundamentally a continual descent into an ever more brittle rigidity of habit (hence "he has a habit" is slang usage for drug addiction). Excess does not recognize the bounds of flow. It demands exact quantities at exact times. Flow is acceptance of whatever comes. As the well-worn AA phrase has it, for the alcoholic "one drink is too many and a thousand never enough." While total abstinence is required from the alcoholic for successful recovery, they are very often predisposed to excesses of other kinds, particularly with food and sex, the desires for which Seneca gives us a prescription here. Alcoholics relating the stories of their recovery in speaker meetings frequently relate how they experienced intense hunger cravings, particularly for sugar, in early sobriety. This is both physiological and psychological. Alcohol is turned mostly into sugar by the body as it is broken down. The craving for sweets is nearly universal for newcomers. But many also talk of excessive food intake. The craving for excess may persist even when the alcoholic has put the plug in the jug. I myself ate between a half-pint and a full pint of Ben and Jerry's every night for the first two years of my sobriety, only avoiding massive weight gain by a counterbalancing rededication to an intensive physical training program that was part of my new disciplined lifestyle. Sex is also often extremely problematic for those in early recovery. Individuals whose drinking took them to the point where they often no longer cared for their appearance or health and spent most of their time isolated may find that, cleaned-up and returned to healthy habits such as exercise, they now attract positive attention from potential sexual partners. It is far too easy to fall into a substitute sexual chase and conquest addiction pattern for many. In fact, it is an unofficial rule of AA that the newly sober person ought not engage in any new intimate relationships for the first year of their sobriety. If they are married, they certainly can carry on with sex with their spouse. But if they are single, they should assiduously avoid sexual and/or romantic entanglements. This seems too much to ask for some, but I have personally heard an awful lot of relapse stories that began with the dissolution of a relationship begun far too early on in the recovery process.

For Seneca, the advice to restrain appetites within natural boundaries and in accordance with the *mos maiorum* ("the ways of the ancestors") serves as prelude to the actual arrival of the ship of soul metaphor:

> Non potest umquam tanta varietas et iniquitas casuum ita depelli, ut non multum procellarum irruat magna armamenta pandentibus.
>
> It is impossible for such a great variety and unfairness of misfortune to be repulsed so that many gales won't rush down upon those leaving their sails wide open to the wind.
>
> (*De Tranq.* IX.3)

The metaphor provides a vivid image of *tranquillitas* as achieved by a hedging against *fortuna* achieved by the minimization of fortune's opportunities to inflict damage on an individual Stoic's psychology. The dangers inherent to sailing with sheets open to the wind invoke the kind of *tempestas* that is to be avoided while simultaneously emphasizing that this is not a picture of elimination of fortune's influence indicated in a withdrawal to a *mare mortuum* ("a dead sea"), i.e., a complete removal of oneself from the hazards of life. Seneca elsewhere writes of this life that resembles "a dead sea" and makes clear that such a life does not qualify as *tranquillitas*, but rather *malacia* ("a dead calm"), suggestive of a becalmed sea rather than a smooth flow.[12] This is a critical distinction because it is one that Serenus does not seem to grasp in the opening of Seneca's treatise since the first time the term *tranquillitas* is utilized within the text, prior to Seneca's selection of it as his chosen term for Stoic *euthymia*, it is clearly used to indicate a complete withdrawal from life as made clear by the phrase "*expers publicae privataeque curae*" ("having no part in affairs public or private").[13] Serenus also indicates that it is not a settled psychological state but rather an extreme opposed by the contrary impulse the next moment to hurl himself into the midst of public business in the Forum.[14] Seneca's treatise, then, is in part a correction of Serenus' perspective on what constitutes true *tranquillitas*. This mild correction of Serenus' ethical misunderstanding accords with Serenus' statement at the close of his *proemium* or introduction to the letter that he is a drowning man, albeit one drowning "in sight of land" (*in conspectu terrarum*).[15]

Seneca is aiming, then, to correct the faulty perspective of his philosophical sponsee. Serenus is prone to all-or-nothing thinking, seeing only complete engagement or complete detachment as options. AAs are known to operate from such one thing-or-another-type thinking in recovery. Some are so attracted by the allure of a newly opened spiritual path in their lives that they pursue it to the exclusion of more practical matters. Humorous anecdotes about *dharma* contemplation in the dark since the electric bill hasn't been paid have been heard in AA meetings. Others tack too far in the opposite direction, focusing on acquiring all the material things their drinking either prevented them from having or took away from them, especially a new car, a new house, and a mate.[16] AA sponsors frequently refer their sponsees to one of the quotes found on placards in most meeting halls, "Easy Does It," reminding them not to get too carried away in any one direction in their lives. One certainly can enrich their spiritual life while still taking care of household tasks and responsibilities. And one can cultivate tranquility while sailing some very choppy waters. But these things must be done gradually, deliberately, and in as low stress an environment as possible. The sponsee who, like Serenus, sees only complete withdrawal or total engagement might be prompted to break up with their partner, sell their apartment, and sign up to live at a Buddhist monastery three months into sobriety. This dramatic change of life is, as one can easily imagine, not the kind that usually serves well as a long-term spiritual path.

The ship of soul metaphor acts as a consistent thread weaving together Seneca's varied psychological recommendations for emotion regulation in sections 9 through 14 of his treatise. It is here where technique resonates consistently with the metaphoric term chosen for the very concept upon which the treatise centers.[17] The metaphor is picked up again at X.6, where Seneca further elucidates just how a Stoic can place limits on the dangers to which Fortune is wont to subject him:

> Nihil tamen aeque nos ab his animi fluctibus vindicaverit, quam semper aliquem incrementis terminum figere, nec fortunae arbitrium desinendi dare.
>
> Finally, nothing redeems us as much from fluctuations of the mind as the fixing of a certain limit to growth and to not leave to fortune the decision of putting an end to it.
>
> (*De Tranq.* X.6)

Seneca's emphasis on the establishment of limits to our desires and engagements for the goal of tranquility is found also in Marcus Aurelius, who reinterprets a Democritean aphorism, Ὀλίγα πρῆσσε, φησίν, εἰ μέλλεις εὐθυμήσειν ("Do a little, he said, if you intend to be to be in good spiritual condition"), for Stoics as the fulfillment of the necessary social and political duties with the recognition that most of our words and actions are in fact not necessary.[18] This is Greek philosophy's very own "Easy Does It" slogan. As Hadot observes of Marcus' application of Democritus' handy slogan for obtaining *euthymia*, "It is not, as Democritus seems to say, the mere fact of reducing the number of one's actions which brings serenity, or the fact of not getting involved in many things, but the fact of limiting one's activities to that which serves the common good."[19] In the Senecan context, the advice to Serenus of the "fixing of a limit" to one's political ambitions in "terminum figere" speaks to the same understanding of *euthymia*, vivified through the imagery of the sailing metaphor and its tie to his chosen term for *euthymia*, *tranquillitas*.

Specific psychological techniques elucidated through metaphor: *Praemediatio Malorum* or "Rehearsal of Misfortunes" in Seneca and "a design for living that works in rough going."[20]

Seneca next activates the metaphor in an elucidation of Stoic acceptance of reality, in relation to two specific Stoic psychological strategies discussed in our previous chapter, namely *praemeditatio malorum* and *hupexhairesis*. *Praemeditatio malorum* is a strategy advocated by the Stoics, especially Seneca and Epictetus, for engaging purposefully in the contemplation of "disasters" that might likely befall one in life, from disease and accident to financial ruin and political exile. The aim of such a meditation exercise is the strengthening of one's understanding that all of these possible disasters are in fact not evils at all, but rather indifferents.[21] *Hupexhairesis*, the Stoic "reserve clause," is a kind of flipside to *praemeditatio malorum* in which one meditates on one's aims in life, but practices adding an "if fate permits" caveat to all of one's endeavors.[22] Instead of allowing oneself to be taken fully by imagining the fulfillment of aims, the Stoic reminds themself of all the things outside of their control that might stand in the way, and the ultimately indifferent status of all targets vis-à-vis the true *telos* of serenity.[23] The beauty of Seneca's versions of these Stoic psychotherapeutic techniques as explicated in *De Tranquillitate Animi* is his creative working out of them through the metaphor of the ship of soul. The metaphor provides coherence to the ethical prescriptions, rendering a portrait of the techniques applied.

The ship of soul sets sail from birth onto a sea of disasters. Seneca extends the metaphor from the dangers of the sea to the dangers inherent to all human life, designating these dangers our "crewmates" in life:

> Morbus est, captivitas, ruina, ignis; nihil horum repentinum est: sciebam, in quam tumultuosum me contubernium natura cluisset.
>
> There is sickness, captivity, ruin, fire; none of these things comes suddenly: I knew it all along, with what tumultuous company nature shut me in.
>
> (*De Tranq.* XI.7)

By applying the same adjective, *tumultuosus* ("full of tumult"), which Serenus had earlier used at I.17 to describe the more greatly disturbed mental state associated with true *tempestas* to the crewmates of the soul, Seneca makes clear that potential disturbances are part and parcel of human life. It is the aim of Stoic ethics to help us toward the acceptance of ever-present disaster. In effect the state of *tempestas* results for Seneca from a failure to properly recognize and accept the inherent nature of human existence.[24] Nature does not actually throw us with shocks and surprises unless we fail to fully acknowledge the crewmates on our own ship of soul.[25] *Praemeditatio malorum* can help us by ensuring we are ready and waiting so we are not taken off guard and plunged into *tempestas*, for disasters do not come out of nowhere—"*nihil horum repentinum est*" ("none of these things come suddenly"). To sail the sea of life as a Stoic is to expect storm. The Stoic can thus obtain *tranquillitas* in the very midst of the *tempestas*.

From the Stoic perspective the principal ethical failing of most people lies in their failure through neglect or refusal to acknowledge the ubiquity and frequency of the dangers inherent to our existence, erroneously excepting themselves from the misfortunes that befall others. They manage somehow to blind themselves with a "well, that won't happen to me" perspective. Seneca is mystified by this phenomenon, which he makes a point of very shortly after the *contubernium* ("crewmate") passage cited above:

> Mirer ad me aliquando pericula accessisse, quae circa me semper erraverint? Magna pars hominum est, quae navigatura de tempestate non cogitat.
>
> Should I marvel that dangers which wander around me at all times sometimes approach me? The great majority of humanity does not contemplate storm when it is about to set sail.
>
> (*De Tranq*. XI.8)

Part of aiming for *tranquillitas* in the navigation of life is the acknowledgment of the likelihood of *tempestas*. In order to maintain *tranquillitas*, every action must be undertaken with a potential storm in mind. Seneca has explicated the therapeutic value of the Stoic practice of *praemeditatio malorum* through the metaphor of the ship of soul, giving greater force to his rendering of *euthymia* as *tranquillitas* in the process.[26]

So how exactly can a recovering person benefit from the practice of *praemeditatio malorum*? Though it will prove to be useful throughout recovery, *praemeditatio malorum* would seem to have a special relevance to combating one of the dangers to long-term recovery most often experienced by those in early recovery, namely the infamous period known in AA as "The Pink Cloud." Not every early AA member experiences this phase, but a great number of them do to varying degrees. It is the euphoric feeling that can accompany finally getting clean. Being sick and tired from continual abuse of mind and body via alcohol and/or other drugs does not leave many people feeling too healthy physically and mentally upon first coming into the rooms. Those in early recovery find their appetite restored and become healthier by eating better. They are often getting good sleep for the first time in many years. Many also begin exercise routines that provide the natural high of endorphins released by the body alongside the confidence of feeling capable and looking better. "The Pink Cloud" can be dangerous in that it may make recovery seem easier than it in fact is by allowing the recovering individual to push away thoughts of just how difficult life without the numbing effects of alcohol is. Many an alcoholic has given essentially the same narrative of relapse, which goes something like the following: I finally stopped drinking and felt great. I cleared up my legal problem by actually doing what I needed to do. I started to perform better at work. I started working out. I met a nice person. But then "life got lifey," i.e., challenges came my way. I tore my Achilles tendon and couldn't exercise. The relationship didn't work out. I started to feel depressed. I stopped going to meetings. I wasn't calling my sponsor any longer. I went to a destination wedding and before I even knew what happened I was downing Rum Swizzles on a Bermuda beach. A wise sponsor might well suggest a homespun version of *praemeditatio* by reminding a new sponsee of all the things that can go wrong in one's life and how real recovery is about not drinking "no matter what." By contemplating in advance challenges they may face, the newly recovering person builds up their resilience so that if their Pink Cloud suddenly turns into a thunderstorm one day six months into recovery, they won't react with the default search for a way to numb what they are feeling but rather respond as they contemplated they might via *praemediatio*. One of the intrinsic beauties of Seneca's metaphor is its deep applicability to the trajectory of life. As on a sea voyage, there will be calm and pleasant days, becalmed and restive days, days of choppy waters and emotional nausea, and days of legitimate storm and the *Sturm und Drang* of life.

Specific Psychological Techniques Elucidated through Metaphor: *Hupexhairesis* or "The Reserve Clause" in Seneca and Following "God's Will" in AA

At the start of section 13 of his treatise on serenity of mind Seneca invokes Democritus and his aphorism about "doing little," discussed above in relation to Marcus Aurelius' citing of it, in a Latin translation in which the phrase *tranquille vivere* ("to live serenely") takes place of the Greek verb εὐθυμήσειν ("to be in good spiritual condition"). Seneca now combines the ethical advice of limiting one's engagement from earlier with the recognition of ever-present danger to formulate within his own metaphor a version of the Stoic "reserve clause." He recommends engaging in self-talk with the repetition of *nisi si* ("unless") clauses in the contemplation of one's goals:

> "Navigabo, nisi si quid inciderit" et "Praetor fiam, nisi si quid obstiterit" et "Negotio mihi respondebit, nisi si quid intervenerit."
>
> "I will sail, unless something happens" and "I will become praetor, unless something stands in the way." And "Affairs will go my way, unless something intervenes."
>
> (*De Tranq.* XIII.2)

In isolation, the first example of self-talk might be speaking only about an actual trip. But within the context of the construction of the metaphor throughout the text, Seneca clearly imparts to it a more generalized meaning. All the things we aim at should be treated as if they were scheduled sea journeys, susceptible to postponement or cancellation depending on the weather, a factor outside of our *hegemonikon*'s control. The structure of the three examples is also indicative. Seneca proceeds from a specific example that is generalized through the metaphor to a specific example to a final general example. He thus evokes the general through images of the metaphor and then closes with a general example after providing a very specific intervening example from the realm of Roman politics.

Bill Wilson, in composing the first 164 pages of the book *Alcoholics Anonymous*, was keenly aware of the wisdom of the "reserve clause" in central areas of the recovering individual's life, namely with respect to their career and their work in helping other alcoholics. The recovering alcoholic may be especially vulnerable to thinking in overly positive ways that, in all probability, don't match up with reality. The overwhelming enthusiasm for life that often naturally accompanies the AA member's recovery from "a hopeless state of mind and body"[27] renders them susceptible to thinking everything will work out well from here on out. In other words, alcoholics, especially newly sober ones, are prone to thinking that alcohol alone stood in the way of all their dreams coming true. Unfortunately, this is not the case, as those with longer-term recovery will inform anyone who asks (perhaps with an accompanying chuckle as they recall their early days). Let us consider a job/career scenario first off. The now-sober alcoholic might think that better performance in their current job or the starting of the new job beckons them to great things, but they might be forgetting that the company and the boss do not share the reborn-from-the-dead perspective of the alcoholic. Bill gives the following sage advice:

> I'm glad you are going to try that new job. But make sure that you are only going to "try." If you approach the project in the attitude that "I must succeed, I must not fail, I cannot fail," then you practically guarantee the flop which in turn will guarantee a drinking relapse. But if you look at the venture as a constructive experiment only, then all should go well.[28]

Bill takes the "reserve clause" idea a step further here in noting the psychological trap of operating without it. Repeating to oneself regularly, "I will succeed in this new project/new job, if the conditions are suitable for me and the company," makes proper use of the Stoic wisdom.

Another area in which recovering individuals often find themselves operating without a healthy "reserve clause" is in trying to get others sober. Filled with enthusiasm for recovery, they are in danger of forgetting that no one got them sober, but rather they finally made a different choice. The AA dictum is: "You alone can do it, but you cannot do it alone." Wise old-timers who have done a good amount of sponsoring will often offer the advice to "detach with love" from a sponsee who just isn't putting forward the effort recovery requires. A sponsor ought to approach the sobriety of a sponsee with a reserve clause built in as follows: I will do everything I can to help guide this person in their recovery, unless they decide they do not want sobriety and recovery.

Those with a Christian background or knowledge of the Middle Ages might think of the phrase *deo volente* ("God willing") here, the most repeated phrase of all of medieval Europe. This phrase is also a form of the "reserve clause," a way of reminding oneself that in any endeavor or undertaking the outcome is not up to us. The "reserve clause" is then a very helpful way of living in Epictetus' distinction between what is up to us and what isn't from Chapter 1. The planning, the effort put forth, etc., are in our power. The outcome is not. Keeping this in mind makes it much easier to focus on process rather than outcome and "to stay in the day," as AAs formulate it.

Contemplating the Sage

In keeping with Stoic practice, Seneca proceeds to provide specific *exempla* or "models" from the lives of sages or near sages.[29] The three *exempla* listed are highly suggestive of Seneca's purposes. He begins with a Greek—Zeno, the founder of the Stoic school—and concludes with a Roman from his own lifetime, bridging the gap with a Greek philosopher in an equivalent political position to contemporary Romans. The connection to the development of the metaphor is found in Zeno's story. Here the dangers of shipwreck, so far metaphorical, are literalized:

> Nuntiato naufragio Zenon noster, cum omnia sua audiret submersa: "Iubet," inquit, "me fortuna expeditius philosophari."
>
> After it was announced that the ship was wrecked, when our Zeno heard that all his possessions had sunk, he said, "Fortune orders me to philosophize more unencumbered."
>
> (*De Tranq.* XIV.3)

In literal shipwreck Zeno, the original Stoic, becomes the *exemplum* of employing the full psychological *armamentarium* of tranquility. His reaction assumes shipwreck a probability of sea travel for which *praemeditatio malorum* has prepared him. His acceptance of reality, of *fortuna*, reveals a complete understanding of what is and isn't within his control. His favorable, even joking, interpretation of his misfortune turns shipwreck into an advantageous freeing of himself from encumbrances.[30]

Theodorus comes as the next exemplum of the Stoic's tranquility in a standard philosopher versus tyrant standoff, where the philosopher's indifference to the plight of his body trumps the worst threat—inhumation while alive—the tyrant can conjure against him. But it is the third and final exemplum, that of Julius Canus, through which Seneca succeeds in weaving together the sage's outlook with the specific political plight of Romans like himself who are charged with maintaining tranquility under murderous emperors. Canus' shipwreck is in the worst of political storms, the principate of Caligula. Canus' tranquility of mind is succinctly conveyed through his response to the confirmation that the order for his execution has been given: "Gratias," inquit, "ago, optime princeps" ("I thank you, best ruler," he said). Seneca proceeds to contemplate exactly the nature of the jest Canus is making at the emperor's expense, but this is only the beginning of Canus' playful treatment of his pending execution. While awaiting his death free from any anxiety, Canus occupies himself by playing chess. Summoned to his death, he insists that his playing partner not attempt to claim victory because the centurion stands as witness that Canus was winning the final game. To his tearful friends, Canus, like a Roman Socrates, gives the philosopher's answer that he will be the first to learn the truth about death.[31] In this way he turns his death into an experiment in the process of dying that he intends to observe as long as possible, and report back to his friends the results of his investigation. Seneca steps out of his own telling of the story at this moment to point out Canus for observation and recognition by his readers:

> Ecce in media tempestate tranquillitas, ecce animus aeternitate dignus, qui fatum suum in argumentum veri vocat, qui in ultimo illo gradu positus exeuntem animam percontatur nec usque ad mortem tantum sed aliquid etiam ex ipsa morte discit. Nemo diutius philosophatus est.
>
> Behold! Tranquility in the very midst of storm, behold! A mind worthy of eternity, which called its own death in as proof of truth, which situated on the very last step of life tested its exiting life spirit and learned not only up to the point of death but from death itself. No one has philosophized longer.
>
> (*De Tranq.* 14.10)

This is Seneca's grand conclusion not only to his three Stoic exemplars but also to the first section of his treatise. The phrase "*in media tempestate tranquillitas*" ("'serenity' in the very midst of storm") serves a couple of functions: first, it acknowledges the etymological source of the term Seneca chose for Stoic *euthymia* by directly juxtaposing it to its opposite term in the metaphor so that we see serenity as *the* good spiritual condition opposed to the storm of psychological turmoil; second, it corrects Serenus' misapplication of *tranquillitas* to a life *expers publicae privataeque curae* in the opening of the treatise. The true Stoic aims to achieve *tranquillitas* in the midst of a full engagement with life, not in retreat from it. Immediately after this passage the *animus* of Canus is praised, making for the pointed placement of *tranquillitas* next to *animus* with only the interjection *ecce* intervening, as if to say, here it is, the personified version of the treatise *De Tranquillitate Animi* itself, the man who is the text you are reading. Seneca's treatment of Julius Canus thus combines Socrates' treatment of his pending execution with Stoic ideals and the Roman cultural imperative of resistance to tyranny.

Recovering members of Alcoholics Anonymous also hold up serenity amid turmoil as one of the highest aims of a life guided by the program. But critically AA has no sages, since everyone remains just one drink away from ruin, just another drunk in the group of drunks. With that being said, however, there is no doubt that those newer in recovery look closely at and often contemplate the behavior of those with very long periods of sobriety. Since in the vast majority of cases members with twenty, thirty, and forty or more years in recovery are also dealing with the aging process and all of its challenges, younger members have the opportunity to observe closely the serenity of old-timers in the midst of the emotional storms arising from the death of spouse, a cancer diagnosis, a stroke, and the like. Just as Seneca does not expect Serenus to be the sage that Julius Canus was, so too the person with ten years in recovery is not expected to possess the almost preternatural calm of some old-timers when facing potentially overwhelming psychological and emotional challenges. But as the Stoic can contemplate the sage, so the AA member can marvel at the old-timers in the room who maintain such a sense of acceptance and peace even as the starkest challenges of aging confront them. I have personally experienced this by spending time in a few hospital rooms of dying alcoholics in recovery.

Making Use of Metaphor as a Philosophy of Life in Recovery

Having examined Seneca's use of *tranquillitas* within his construction of the ship of soul metaphor, it is important to consider what is unique about Seneca's employment of metaphor and to both contextualize and analyze it in terms of common uses of metaphor and a richer engagement with metaphor as part of a process of developing specific philosophical content. Illuminating here is an instance where Marcus Aurelius invokes the ship of soul in a simile:

> Ὅτι πάντα ὑπόληψις καὶ αὕτη ἐπὶ σοί. ἆρον οὖν ὅτε θέλεις τὴν ὑπόληψιν καὶ ὥσπερ κάμψαντι τὴν ἄκραν γαλήνη, σταθερὰ πάντα καὶ κόλπος ἀκύμων.
>
> [Know] that opinion is everything and it is itself up to you. Get rid of the opinion whenever you want and just like for the person doubling his course around the headland there will be calm, every kind of stability, and a waveless bay.

Here Marcus, like Seneca, combines an imagistic rendering of Stoic *euthymia* and *tranquillitas* within a ship of soul metaphor. The philosophical concepts within the Senecan term *tranquillitas* are discretely listed, with calm, stability, and freedom from disturbance each getting their own terms. Where Seneca had sought a Latin term to combine all these components of the Stoic *telos* of serenity, Marcus has no single term of this kind available to him. Seneca's *tranquillitas* succeeds in synthesizing in one Latin term three philosophical ideals.

Smith concludes that *tranquillitas* for Seneca "more often represents an amalgamation of different philosophical concepts (*apatheia*, *galena*, and *euthymia*)." As far as analyzing how an inherently metaphorical term accomplishes this, we might consider Stanford's carefully elaborated description of the process of metaphor:

> Metaphor is the process and result of using a term (X) normally signifying an object or concept (A) in such a context that it must refer to another object or concept (B) which is distinct enough in characteristics from A to ensure that in the composite idea formed by the synthesis of the concepts A and B and now symbolized in the word X, the factors A and B retain their conceptual independence while they merge in the unity symbolized by X.
>
> As an example, we might call the best salesman at the car dealership a "homerun hitter." In doing so we have taken a term from baseball and applied it to car sales. Having once done this application of the term from baseball to something else we have created the notion of "homerun hitter" as a top performer in any area. This is the unity of X.[32]

Seneca adds a C element to this definition by working out through a related metaphor, the ship of soul, his metaphorical usage of *tranquillitas*. Marcus makes a more straightforward use of simile and metaphor to illustrate a philosophical point about how Stoics can always locate serenity by controlling their opinions. Seneca's use of *tranquillitas* within the ship of soul metaphor, on the other hand, is formulated philosophically through the metaphorical language. His metaphors create a particular version of Stoic moral psychology in which his chosen term, rich with metaphorical entailments of its own, operates within the extended ship of soul metaphor to arrive at the paradox of *tranquillitas* in the midst of *tempestas*. For Seneca, the metaphor is inherent to his choice of philosophical vocabulary. As Lakoff and Johnson have shown, "metaphorical entailments characterize the internal systematicity of the metaphor" and "make coherent all the examples which fall under the metaphor."[33] It is worthwhile to think this through step by step. Seneca offers in the choice of *tranquillitas* a metaphorical term for the Stoic *telos* of peace of mind, which contains multiple key philosophical concepts, all having their starting point in the etymological origins of the term employed in Latin for calm sea. The central fact of calm sea is that it is good for a ship to sail upon, including the metaphorical ship of soul. The entailment, then, is that the Stoic ship of soul seeks *tranquillitas*. The subsequent metaphorical entailment is that psychological disturbance is either a *fluctatio* or *tempestas*, or presumably most often somewhere in between. But the critical moment comes with the paradoxical twist Seneca adds to the metaphors, showing that once the *tranquillitas* is properly internalized, the *tempestas* can rage while *tranquillitas* is maintained. A Stoic soul, then, is a ship capable of sailing on a tranquil sea despite stormy conditions. Here we might modify C. Day Lewis's assessment of how metaphors function: "We find poetic truth struck out by the collision rather than the collusion of images."[34] If we change poetic to philosophical, we approach a deeper understanding of how Seneca philosophizes in the Latin language by building to the juxtaposition of *tranquillitas* and *tempestas*.

These are, admittedly, deep waters of language and symbol to swim in (play on words very much intended). It may be fair to ask what the recovering person can take away from this deep dive into the machinery of metaphor. One purpose is to reflect on the ubiquity of metaphor itself in all our lives as a way of conjuring truths through images, and thus recommending becoming more aware of the way one pictures their sobriety, both physical and emotional. Does the recovering person's meditation practice create for them something akin to Seneca's *tranquillitas in tempestate*? The ability to say "I am okay" regardless of the circumstances one finds oneself in is a core psychological aim of recovery, after all. *Picturing* the separateness of oneself from the condition or situation they find themself in may well be the best route to a healthy relationship with ourselves and external events. Consider as an example the language and imagery of the following mediation from one of the Hazelden series daily meditation books:

> Today, I will remember that the frustrations around me are not all of who I am. When I am at peace within, I live among spiritual riches.[35]

Alternatively, we might put it as what a long-term recovering man said to his therapist: "*Right now my life is a mess, but* I'm *fine*."[36]

The sense of awareness of the deep separateness between one's true self and one's circumstances is at the heart of Stoic wisdom and the insights of the journey of recovery.

What Seneca offers us beyond this wisdom is a way of painting a word picture of the wisdom in action. The value of this seems to me to lie in how a life rendered in pictures is more open to the inevitability of *tempestas* and thus more accepting, and subsequently more serene. If *tempestas* is always part of the picture, we are prepared in advance to sail through it as something expected. Consider the following reflection, also found in the Hazelden meditation reader, on the following Oliver Wendell Holmes quote: "Life is painting a picture, not doing a sum":

> When our lives are lived as rich and interesting pictures, we find our rewards are far deeper and more lasting. May the picture I paint today be one I will carry with me and appreciate.[37]

If I paint the picture, I create the narrative, reaffirming for myself that it is not the events that happen to me but the attitude I have toward them, the story I tell about them, and my response to them that are the determinants of my happiness. If I conceptualize the picture as something I carry in my head, I separate myself from it, allowing myself to maintain my *tranquillitas* even if the portion of the picture I am painting now is of a turbulent *tempestas*.

Figure 3. Bust of Marcus Aurelius, 2nd century CE. Credit: Ephesus Archaeological Museum in Selçuk, Turkey, Public Domain.

4

Nature as Higher Power in Recovery

The Philosophical Imagery of Marcus Aurelius' *Meditations* and the *Tao Te Ching*

At a couple of earlier junctures, we briefly encountered Marcus Aurelius (121–180 CE) and his *Meditations*. Marcus, having been the Emperor of Rome and the only legitimate incarnation of the Philosopher Ruler whom Plato (427–347 BCE) envisioned in his *Republic*, is without doubt the most well-known of all the Stoics, and his book of daily contemplations for living the philosophical life is far and away the most widely read of all Stoic works. Much less well-known is that Marcus promulgates few philosophical ideas of his own, almost everything having to do with Stoic ethics being drawn directly from Epictetus. What Marcus does add to Epictetus is a spiritual depth of reflection; and he does this primarily through the way in which he represents nature and its role in our ethical lives. He is not the brilliant writer Seneca is, but he is an imagistic thinker who carefully elucidates the union of *logos* (reason) and *phusis* (nature) at the heart of the Stoic perspective more powerfully than anyone before or after him. Epictetus provides the schematics and the reasoning behind the idea of a life in accordance with nature; Marcus has his reader touch and smell a tree and contemplate the connection of their life to it.

In the pages to follow, I will show how we might best understand the centrality of the role of observing and following nature in Stoicism through delving into Marcus' poetically inspired images by comparing them with markedly similar ones from the *Tao Te Ching* of Laozi (traditionally sixth century BCE). In comparing the two world philosophies of Stoicism and Taoism, we shall find injunctions to begin or enhance a meditative practice that opens the way to a conception of a Higher Power to those in search of one in recovery, or to those having an existing one but perhaps looking to enrich it.

In the previous chapter we also focused much on philosophical imagery and closed with a meditation from the Hazelden series. It seems reasonable to start from where we left off by looking at another highly relevant recovery meditation quote. This one comes from Pablo Casals, renowned cellist, composer, and conductor:

> In music, in the sea, in a flower, in a leaf, in an act of kindness ... I see what people call God in all these things.[1]

Putting aside the first item in the list as the default for a composer and cellist, the next three items here—namely sea, flower, and leaf—all speak to the fundamental Stoic understanding of nature as the true expression of the divine rationality that pervades the universe. Seeing god in these is what Marcus urges himself (the proper title of the *Meditations* is, in fact, *To Himself*) and his readers to do. So let us embark on a journey wherein the observance of nature is the contemplation of a Higher Power, or God.

A Structural Parallelism: *Logos* and *Phusis* in the *Meditations* and *Tao* and *Ziran* in the *Tao Te Ching*

In Greco-Roman Stoicism the guiding principle of all things in the universe is the *logos*, reason or the rational element of the universe. The *logos* pervades both human nature *qua* rational animal and nature as a whole. Two brief quotations from the *Meditations* sufficiently illustrate this:

> One essence and one law, the *logos* common to all animals possessing intellect. (7.9)[2]
>
> All matter is soon made to disappear into the essence of the whole and everything responsible for its existence is taken back into the *logos* of the whole.
>
> (7.10)

The Greek term for nature is *phusis*, and Stoicism makes following *phusis* the central ethical injunction by which human beings, as the only rational animals in the universe, endeavor to be in alignment with their unique share of the *logos* and with the *logos* of *phusis* itself.[3] As a concrete elucidation of this philosophical conceptualization of the relationship between the human being, *logos*, and *phusis*, consider that at one point Marcus defines a "rebel" as one who "withdraws from the *logos* of *phusis*."[4] In the pages to follow, we will see that the originality of Marcus' Stoicism is found in how he consistently characterizes man's relationship with the *logos* not just through the concept of *phusis*, but most powerfully through the imagery of the natural world itself. It is a procedure of philosophical illustration remarkably similar to that found throughout the *Tao Te Ching*.

The fundamental similarity between the *logos* of Stoicism and the *Tao* in Taoism can and has been illustrated in many ways. My example is from the Chinese translation of the opening of the *Book of John* in the New Testament. The Stoic influence on John's conception of the divine is felt in the famous prologue to the book where "the word" that "is the beginning and is with God and is God" is a translation of *logos* in Greek. The passage is translated into Chinese not haphazardly and with deep understanding of the depth of shared philosophical perspective by Dr. Wu by having *tao* replace *logos*![5] But the similarities go much deeper. Consider section 25 of the *Tao Te Ching*:

> Man follows the ways of the earth;
> Earth follows the ways of Heaven;
> Heaven follows the ways of Tao;
> Tao follows the ways of itself.

"The ways of itself" at the close of this passage is a translation of *ziran*, a term also translated as "nature."[6] *Phusis* in Greek likewise could be rendered as "ways of itself," since it represents that which is inherently natural to a living being. In her analysis of this passage, Yu makes a very convincing argument about how to understand what the relationship is between *tao* and *ziran*:

> What Laozi (i.e. *Dao de Jing*), is saying is that *dao* is characterized by *ziran* and that this should be the right state of human beings, earth, and heaven. To characterize *dao* in terms of *ziran* is the novelty of Daoism. If one simply says that it is the best life to follow *dao*, this is a common premise of ancient Chinese philosophy. Yet, if one says that it is the best life to follow *dao* as *ziran* (nature or naturalness), then we have Daoism.[7]

The recovering person having begun any acquaintance with AA literature or meetings will quickly recognize the injunction to follow God's will and not self-will. Step Three of AA's Twelve Steps reads: "Made a decision to turn our will and our lives over to the care of God *as we understood him*." For those who have struggled with Bill's language in *Alcoholics Anonymous* that points in the direction of a personal, Christian God, the Stoic and Taoist view of nature as god opens a spiritual pathway. This is a naturalistic, nonreligious path of spiritual surrender and acceptance. What does such a path look like?

An Obscure Path

Delving into the poetic images of Marcus' *Meditations* and the *Tao Te Ching* reveals some striking similarities of expression that have some very important philosophical implications. Marcus writes in multiple places of the road or path of virtue that aligns with the *logos*:

> It [i.e., the motion of virtue] has free passage advancing on a path which is hard to understand.
>
> (*Meditations* 6.17)

At another point, Marcus speaks of that which is without *logos* wandering at random, having lost the path. Now compare the imagery applied to the *Tao* in chapter 21:

> As to the Tao itself, It is elusive and evasive, evasive, elusive.

As "Tao" itself is a word with its root meaning in path or way (hence the most common English translation of "The Way"), both Marcus' *Meditations* and the *Tao Te Ching* present their philosophies as following a path that is not easily understood or comprehended. The language of obscurity and elusiveness applied to the path in both texts points to a coherence between image and philosophical message in the style of both texts: most people are lost on another road, one they hope leads to riches, glory, pleasure, or the like. Few are willing to seek along the obscure, dim, and hard way to comprehend the path of true Stoic or Taoist enlightenment.

Individuals with long-term sobriety often speak of how different the path of their lives has become after recovery, far beyond the avoidance of the ultimate consequences of alcoholism, i.e., jails, institutions, and death. Many of the concerns that dominated their lives prior to recovery are replaced by spiritual goals. This is not to say that the AA way of life does not concern itself with practical goals involving employment, family, and the like. After all, as we have seen in this book's first three chapters, the emotional and psychological changes brought about in recovery are all conducive to greater success in these areas.

The recovery path is obscure to many nonalcoholics because it often involves a dynamic shift away from the default societal perspectives on what is important in life. The obscure nature of the new path can baffle family and friends of the recovering person whose priorities have shifted in such a profound way. The key is keeping some sense of balance and a willingness to communicate with partners and friends. The spiritual path does not look identical for any two individuals. But that does not preclude one from analyzing and reflecting upon some of the general similarities of philosophically enlightened spiritual paths from all traditions.

Embracing a spiritual path means primarily that many recovering individuals no longer assess "success" in life as they did before, in terms of high-paying jobs, spouses and children, houses and cars. The inner journey becomes primary for many. Sylvia Carey, whose book *The Alcoholic Man* traces the journeys of a varied group of men through the many stages of recovery, addresses the question, "How spiritual a path?" beautifully by juxtaposing the lives of two men. Each was sober for twenty years, but their recovery paths led one away from a good career toward spiritual enlightenment via yoga, meditation, and a good deal of time spent in India, and the other to a focus on work, love, sex, money, the concerns of what Carey deems "the householder" path in a nod to the Hindu conception of the variety of lives people lead.[8]

What AAs who thrive in recovery seem to know in a deep sense is that whichever path is primary for them, the concerns of the other path must not be neglected. It usually takes years of experimentation in sobriety for each person to find the balance that suits them best. As for the Stoics, it is clear from the style, presentation, and the points of emphasis that Epictetus is an extremely pragmatic thinker whose manner of teaching concerns itself for the most part with one's banal existence; and that Marcus' focus is more upon the cosmic perspective.

Water and the Flow of Life

Those familiar with the *Tao Te Ching* even in a passing way may well recall just how prominent water imagery is within the text. Along with the ravine or valley, water is one of the primary symbols of Taoism, for it is the soft or passive element that overcomes the hard and forcefully active. One particular passage is strikingly evocative of the role of water imagery in Marcus' Stoicism:

> [The spontaneous working of] the *Tao* in the world is like the flow of the valley brooks into a river or sea.
>
> (*Tao Te Ching* 32)

Compare Marcus' poetic simile for Stoic acceptance:

> A disposition welcoming every happening as necessary, as familiar, as *flowing* from just such a source and fount.
>
> (*Meditations* 4.33)

Notably, the Stoics characterized those living a life aligned with the *logos* as "having a good flow of life," *to euroun* in Greek.[9] In fact, the dominant influence on Marcus' own Stoicism, Epictetus, pairs *euroun* with *apathes* as the two primary goals of Stoicism.[10] *Apatheia*, you will recall, is the state of passionless-ness, or elimination of the negative emotions that can overthrow rationality, which leads the Stoic to true serenity and tranquility in life. Marcus chooses to expand the poetic imagery of nature around the concept of good flow to further elucidate the doctrine. Alignment with the *logos* and elimination of the passions that threaten that alignment result in the good flow of life of the virtuous Stoic. The *Tao Te Ching* likens the *tao* itself to water in chapter 8.[11] The person of virtue in both Taoism and Stoicism is then one who lives a flow of life in harmony with the flow of the *tao* or the *logos*.

One of the most central tenets of recovery centers on yielding to the reality around us. As Bill puts it, "We have ceased fighting anyone or anything—even alcohol."[12] When the alcoholic attempts to fight alcohol, they always lose. When they surrender and admit powerlessness, instead of fighting, their energy *flows* in the new direction of recovery. What those who live the recovering life for years come to realize is that what worked on their desperate, self-destructive addiction to alcohol works on life's other problems as well. Learning to flow rather than fight is ceaselessly ethically efficacious. And it resides in the heart of the Stoic and Taoist worldviews. What both philosophies provide is a way to visualize the flow we wish to bring to our lives. The water of the *tao* or *logos* flows gently and smoothly, but there are naturally turbulent waters to be encountered in our lives. How we conceptualize those raging torrents of loss, grief, frustration, and the like, and ourselves in relation to them, is critical to our mental health in recovery. The Stoics and Taoists paint a vivid picture for us to live up to.

In both Marcus' *Meditations* and the *Tao Te Ching* water that is raging or torrential represents the opposite of the *tao* or the *logos*. Here Marcus pictures the man living in accord with nature as the calm in the midst of the storm—the separate, unaffected, still object in the raging sea of life:[13]

> To be like the cape, against which the waves ceaselessly dash: it stands firm and the swollen waves are put to sleep around it.
>
> (*Meditations* 4.49)

Compare a similar image from the *Tao Te Ching*:

> Sudden, like the sea, like a tempest, as though endless, the mass of people all have their means—I alone am obstinate, uncouth. I alone wish to be different from others, and value feeding from the mother.
>
> (Ch. 20)

Both passages exemplify the sage as a figure of stillness and calm, separate and resistant to the surging mass of humanity, driven on as they are by their deluded desires for wealth and prestige, power and authority, the pleasures of sex and food, and the like. Part and parcel of this stillness and calm is the elimination of the raging desires through the cultivation of a pure and clean simplicity of life.

AAs do not need to become Taoist monks and leave society behind in order to live this spiritual path or just benefit from contemplating it. However, all recovery literature does urge the creation of microcosmic versions of the kind of withdrawal, solitude, and stillness envisaged in the Stoic and Taoist imagery. The Eleventh Step is the official locus of the AA approach to the creation of a place and time separate from the world devoted to meditation and contemplation. Most AAs I have known take this time first thing in the morning, but how it looks is widely varied according to the pressures of work, family, health, and more. Some can only squeeze ten minutes before their young children come clamoring into their bedrooms. Others, retired, have the time to find a favorite pleasant spot with a beautiful view of nature and a mocha latte to settle in for a half an hour or more of contemplating meditative readings. Some cultivate more Zen-like practices, meditation not upon readings, but rather guided-meditations moving them toward the embrace of stillness and emptiness. Regardless of the style of meditation, one of the principal psychological benefits is the bringing into being of a sense of self that is still, unshakeable, calm, and separate from the turbulent waters whipped up by the buffeting winds of everyday stressors.

Purity and Cleanliness

Both Stoicism and Taoism emphasize the elimination of the unnecessary, the superfluous, the residue of distractions outside of oneself that hinder the still and gentle state being sought by both philosophies. The *Tao Te Ching* formulates this goal as a question:

> In cleansing and purifying your mystic vision, can you be free from all dross?
>
> (Ch. 10)

Compare how Marcus presents the Stoic goal of self-liberation by means of purification:

> How easily contented is the one who pushes back and wipes away every troublesome or inappropriate appearance and exists in an utterly tranquil sea.
>
> (5.2)

The shared language of cleansing here evokes a state of natural being, before the addition of all the accoutrements of civilization. This is clear in the *Tao Te Ching* as the question above immediately follows one about becoming "as the new-born babe." In a similar vein, Marcus selects the adjective *eukolos* to describe the state resulting from pushing back and wiping away appearances. This adjective has the root meaning of being easily pleased with one's food, thus evoking a very young child satisfied with nourishment prior to the development of personal (dis)tastes.

In a variety of ways, the recovery process also involves a purifying process that entails a stripping away of habits of misperception. The life of addiction is one of skewed and distorted perspectives that become increasingly twisted and tangled in the addict's often grotesquely elaborate attempts to justify a worldview that is compatible with continuing their drinking, the only end goal that matters, despite all the mounting evidence that they need to stop. One of the principal sources of humor in AA meetings is the recognition in a fellow alcoholic's story or share of the utter absurdity of the skewed perceptions and wayward *thinking* that allowed them to keep drinking. To cite one of the most commonly occurring instances of this shared recognition of the misperception that went hand-in-hand with drinking, AA meetings invariably break into laughter whenever a member shares about the utter incomprehensibility of a phenomenon witnessed in a spouse or friend: that of leaving a glass of alcohol half-finished at dinner, a bar, or a party. To come to understand that doing this is reflective of a normal attitude to alcohol and not proof of a person's status as an alien from another planet is a mind-opening experience for the alcoholic. To the nonalcoholic it is the norm.

As discussed earlier, the Twelve Steps are at root a set of cognitive behavioral adaptations. Foundational to any cognitive behavioral change is the realization that one can change one's attitudes by changing their perceptions. In a well-known analogy this process is envisaged as the removing of one's glasses to clean them. This is exactly what Marcus has in mind in asking us to contemplate the wiping away of troublesome appearances in the passage above.

Donald Robertson, a cognitive behavioral therapist who traces the Stoic influence on his field, fleshes out the glasses analogy:

> This is often illustrated by the analogy of wearing coloured spectacles. Normally we view the world "through" the lens of our positive or negative judgements, like someone looking at the world through "rose-tinted" spectacles or through gloomy dark glasses. We may forget we're wearing glasses, though, and assume that's just the way external things look in themselves and how they appear to everyone else. Cognitive distancing is like the process of taking off the glasses and looking at them, rather than through them.[14]

Nature over Art and the Uncarved Block

The specific language of cleansing and purifying as part of a return to the simplicity of an existence prior to the influence of conventional societal values is part of a larger thematic pattern recurrent in both the *Tao Te Ching* and the *Meditations*, one that is centered on the superiority of the natural to the artificial. Here we can see how the microcosmic specifics of the choice of poetic language inform the macrocosmic level of the general ethical injunction "to follow nature" central to both philosophies.[15] Marcus lays this out in the clear terms of philosophical exegesis in contrast to some of the more poetic similes and metaphors we have seen him thus far employ:

> No natural creation is inferior to a work of art, since the arts indeed imitate nature. If this is the case, the most complete and comprehending nature of all other natures cannot be found wanting in comparison with well-crafted art.
>
> (*Meditations* 11.10)

The *Tao Te Ching* continually emphasizes the same philosophical perspective through one of its most famous and dominant images, that of the uncarved block.

> He finds contentment in constant virtue,
> He returns to the uncarved block. (Ch. 28)

Several passages, such as the one below, address the danger inherent in carving or cutting the block:

> Once the block is cut, names appear. When names begin to appear, know then that there is time to stop. It is by this knowledge that danger may be avoided.
>
> (Ch. 32)

The uncarved block is the dominant image of nature prior to the application of craft. In contemplating it, one sees how simple yet complete it is. Statues of Laozi were themselves fashioned to resemble natural formations in harmony with their topographical surroundings, so that they would appear as if part of the natural world rather than works of art made to stand out from it.

The Stoics weren't the Cynics with their extreme ethic of the abandonment of civilized custom and return to animal nature; but they were born as a kind of hybrid child of Socrates (*c.* 470–399 BCE) and Diogenes (*c.* 413–324 BCE), the most well-known Cynic.[16] This is especially true of Epictetus, Marcus' chief influence.[17] He is highly distrustful of much of the artifice of society, high society in particular. Epictetus did not abandon his drinking cup, seeing that a child was utilizing his cupped hands, as Diogenes did. This extreme return to the natural the Stoics left to the Cynics. But he did find a simple clay vessel superior to vessels of greater artifice. Marcus and the other Roman Stoics would certainly have embraced the philosophical implications of the uncarved block, for its shared ideal of a simplicity closest to nature and most devoid of the artifice of man.

The *Tao*'s greater proximity to the natural, as opposed to that created by art or craft, and Marcus' corresponding evaluation of the superiority of nature to art, point to a shared ethic of simplicity that manifests itself within both texts, and in Taoism and Stoicism more generally. Acting and doing are not inherently valuable in either philosophy, since contemplating the uncarved block is superior to carving it. Both point, rather, to the excess of doing and action in most lives. Marcus turns to an aphorism by the pre-Socratic philosopher Democritus (*c.* 460–370 BCE) that we have discussed in another context earlier. Here he gives a more fully fleshed-out, Stoic interpretation:[18]

> "If you are to be of cheerful disposition, do less." Or perhaps better, do what is necessary and just so many things as the *logos* of an animal social by nature demands and as it demands; indeed this brings a cheerful disposition not only from doing things well but also from doing the few essential things.
>
> (*Meditations* 4.24)

This is another instance in which Marcus defines the *logos* in terms of *phusis*, in this case the specific *phusis* of human beings as social animals, a core tenet of the Stoic ethical foundation. For Marcus, human beings spend much of their time doing and acting outside of the requirements of the *logos*, putting themselves at odds with their natural selves. A desire to earn money to buy luxury items is a suitable example. Here a person does more, but because they are driven by a desire for unnatural pleasures, their actions do not harmonize with their nature, and thus, the *logos*.

Marcus' injunction here is not dissimilar to the Taoist ethic of *wuwei*, one of the more difficult concepts of the *Tao Te Ching* for many to comprehend:

> Tao invariably does nothing (*wuwei*),
> And yet there is nothing that is not done.
> And further:
> To win the world one must attend to nothing,
> When one attends to this and that,
> He will not win the world. (Ch. 37)

Wuwei, often translated as above as "doing nothing" or "inaction," is not an ethic of the absence of action, but rather one centered on the elimination of unnecessary action along the lines Marcus speaks of above. The man in harmony with the *tao* will not seek to do *something*, but rather naturally do what is essential. Machek (2015) has convincingly elucidated the perspectives on freedom shared by Taoism and Stoicism in just these terms, namely the freedom that comes from doing only necessary things.[19]

In what sense can contemplation of the do less or inaction wisdom of Stoicism and Taoism benefit the recovering alcoholic? Let us consider in this vein the following description of the addictive personality from Victor La Cerva, a medical doctor and public health expert who has authored a book of meditations for those on a recovery path:

> Various research has identified characteristics of the addictive personality. These include a tendency toward impulsive behavior and seeking a rush of excitement that, at the moment, seems irresistible—to hell with our stated goals and commitments.

The ethical injunction to "do less" is one against the impulse to action. To "do less" is to choose reflectively what few things are really worth doing and then to do them very deliberately. Without question, this kind of restriction on acting is very helpful for alcoholics and other addicts in recovery. AA has an unwritten but well-known "rule," mentioned briefly back in this book's first chapter, about not really changing the surroundings of one's life for the first year of recovery. Don't move unless it is necessitated. Stay married, but don't get married. Stay divorced, but don't get divorced, even if you think you want to. If you still have a job, stay in it. Many alcoholics find these requirements very difficult, as early recovery is immensely exciting and often elicits in the newly recovering person a desire to change everything about their life for the better. The AA wisdom is to focus on the internal change and "do less" about what one's life looks like from the outside. Real and meaningful change is gradual and daily, not running away from one partner to hook up with someone else, or rushing into a relationship when one has been on their own, or overzealously switching careers. La Cerva continues:

> Another trait is a high level of stress and anxiety, part of the drive to find something—*anything*—that will help relieve this uncomfortable state.

The serenity of recovery is not compatible with the absurdities of our "multitasking," always in motion society. To "do less" is to take time for meditation, without anything else going on at the same time. To "do less" is to attend a meeting and really be there, to actively listen and participate, to not be on one's phone. To "do less" is to really prioritize a few things in a day only—recovery first, then perhaps work, and then a meal with the family. It is not creating to-do lists so full that they place additional pressure upon the recovering individual.

Recovery requires a continual change on the psychological and spiritual plane in one's life. There won't be time or energy for attending to too much of "this and that," as the excerpt from the *Tao Te Ching* puts it, if this task is taken seriously. Furthermore, in active alcoholism, the alcoholic is always doing, scheming for ways to fit a life around drinking. To learn to be still is one of the great challenges of recovery at all stages. To come to the realization that in many situations no action might be the best action, since so many factors remain out of the individual's hands, relieves the burden of the obsessive attempt at controlling the uncontrollable that lies deep at the heart of the alcoholic's denial of their disease. A frenetic, "problem-solving" mentality in sobriety is too close kin with the alcoholic way of living. For this reason, "Pause when agitated" is one of the most oft-repeated quotes from the "Big Book." To learn patience and acceptance is the path of "doing less." The disease itself is the ultimate problem without a cure, so getting more efficient at problem-solving is not applicable. We have instead "a daily reprieve."[20]

The Unity of Opposites in the Man of Virtue

In accord with the simplicity and naturalness of the man of virtue is his unification in one person of qualities that are dichotomous in others, qualities that may make of one man either one thing or another, like the block after it is carved, rather than a whole that embraces multiple potentialities like the uncarved block. Both Marcus' *Meditations* and the *Tao Te Ching* formulate this state of potentiality through a unification of opposites in the description of the man of virtue:

> Who can be turbid, yet settling slowly clear?
> Who can be at rest, yet moving slowly come to life? (Ch. 15, *Tao Te Ching*)

Again, the *Tao Te Ching* opts for an illustration of personality through an image from nature, a pool of water disturbed but settling into clarity, thus, in essence, being in neither one state or another. Marcus chooses to put the unity of opposites in more direct terms:

> The man following the *logos* in every way is both leisurely slow and quickly agile simultaneously, both cheery and grave at the same time.
>
> (*Meditations* 10.12a.)

The man in harmony with the *logos* possesses the dichotomous unity of the *logos* just as the man of virtue has those qualities of the *tao* represented by the simultaneity of turbidity and clarity. The lack of commitment to one state or another, the full acceptance of the potentiality of both, is closely tied to two ethical concepts centered on indifference and transformation in both Stoicism and Taoism. Another key Taoist text, the *Zhuangzi*, illustrates the close relation between the unity of opposites and the indifference or lack of preference born of understanding transformation as the fundamental law of nature and *Tao*: "He does not prefer the one or the other. He lets himself be transformed into whatever it may be" (Ch. 6).

The acceptance of all things outside of virtue as "indifferent"—or *adiaphora* in the language of the Stoics, neither good nor bad in their essential nature—is one of the most fundamental tenets of Stoic moral doctrine. The concept of indifferents is founded on the continuous interchange of things that we might erroneously call success and failure, good and bad. These outcomes are not either because they involve many factors outside of our virtuous effort as we will recall from the discussion of the stochastic nature of Stoic virtue in Chapter 2. Marcus himself shows a near obsession with the theme of constant transformation revealed to him through his observation of natural phenomena:

> Contemplate continuously how everything comes into being through change and habituate yourself to consider that the nature of all things cherishes nothing so much as to change existing things and to make new things similar to them.
>
> (*Meditations* 4.36)

The shared approach to the expression of the unity of opposites in Marcus' *Meditations* and the *Tao Te Ching* is a foundational link in the larger set of connections of ethical perspective between Stoicism and Taoism.

We have examined at an earlier juncture the fundamental importance of acceptance in recovery. The unity of opposites ethic provides a specific lens of transformation through which to contemplate acceptance. Not only must we accept our external circumstances in order to find serenity in recovery, but we also must accept our continuously transforming selves. Self-acceptance is becoming a person comfortable with one's own continuously shifting moods and feelings. A low-energy, melancholic mood may not respond to any of the tools of the program. It may just be the self of today. To accept this is to avoid adding frustration and vexation to the melancholy. Can we be melancholy yet serenely accepting? If we want to be successful in recovery, we need to learn how to live the unity of opposites.

5

Time

Seneca and Twenty-Four-Hour-a-Day Living in Recovery

In Chapter 2, one of the weapons of the Stoic *Armamentarium,* which we examined briefly, was delimitation of the present, the therapeutic practice aimed at getting us focused on the here and now.[1] This has its natural corresponding recovery wisdom in the living-one-day-at-a-time approach of AA. In this chapter we will delve more deeply into the ethical perspectives the Stoics held about time and *prosoche* (attention to and awareness of the present moment) through a recovery-oriented close reading of the very first letter of Seneca's intimate and influential *Epistulae Morales* ("Moral Letters"), an urgent exhortation to take possession of one's life by taking possession of one's time through self-examination and a strong desire to make moral progress now.[2] Such an approach makes this chapter unique in this book as we will go through a piece of Stoic philosophy step-by-step as a whole since the letter is quite short, in effect treating the letter as a meditation exercise. Here theory meets practice in a more direct fashion.

Epistulae Morales 1.1

The letter begins thus:

> Ita fac, mi Lucili: vindica te tibi, et tempus quod adhuc aut auferebatur aut surripiebatur aut excidebat collige et serva.
>
> (*EM* 1.1.1)
>
> Act just as you have been, my Lucilius: reclaim yourself on your own behalf, and gather together and preserve your time, which up until now was either being carried off or was slipping away or was falling by the wayside.

The packing together of the four imperative verbs in the opening sentences—*fac* ("act"), *vindica* ("lay claim"), *collige* ("gather together"), and *serva* ("preserve")—is as forceful in its urgent appeal as possible. Seneca's choice of the verb *vindica* (whence "vindicate" in English) calls upon Lucilius, and through him us, to reclaim our very lives in the specific sense of legal property temporarily lost to us. And is it not the case that we too often find ourselves having lost large swaths of time and needing to reclaim them? But to what exactly have we lost our lives? For many, the answer is probably to be found by examining the narcotizing effects of habit and distraction, or perhaps habits of distraction such as those so readily available via cell phone and internet today. Those of us in recovery know all too well exactly what we have lost our time and thus our lives to when still active in our addiction.

Seneca's next words make it abundantly clear that the reclaiming of self *means* the reclaiming of the present moment, the only thing that truly belongs to us in Stoic thought, and which Seneca's legalistic language emphasizes as our property.[3] This is rendered pellucid in the juxtaposition of the words "for yourself" and "time" (*te* and *tempus*) as the objects of imperative verbs that begin and end the sentences respectively.[4] The focus on the insidious ways in which time escapes and we lose it and thus ourselves is made emphatic by the fact that two of three verbs focus on our inattention ("slipping away" and "falling by the wayside"). Seneca thus illustrates the value of *prosoche* as this Stoic practice of vigilant attention will save us from losing time through inattention.

Seneca asks next that we reflect on how time is lost to us to confirm that his view is accurate:

> Persuade tibi hoc sic esse ut scribo: quaedam tempora eripiuntur nobis, quaedam subducunctur, quaedam effluunt.
>
> (*EM* 1.1.1)
>
> Convince yourself that this situation is just as I write of it: certain periods of time are snatched away from us; certain are subtly drawn off; and certain flow away from us. Nevertheless most shameful are the periods of time thrown away because of negligence.

The reclaiming of one's self through the reclaiming of one's time is a process of awakening to an enhanced vigilance about how we live our lives. The loss of that time, which we truly did have within our control but did not utilize well, is the loss of self. Surely everyone, but especially the addict/alcoholic, can identify the great feelings of shame associated with this lost time. Now is the time to do something about it. But what? To begin with, Seneca insists we start really paying attention:

> Et si volueris attendere, magna pars vitae elabitur male agentibus, maxima nihil agentibus, tota vita aliud agentibus.
>
> If you will really pay attention, [you will realize] that a huge part of life glides by for us as we are doing the wrong thing, the largest portion when we are doing nothing, and all of life when we are doing something other [than what we ought to be doing].

It may sound like Seneca is dishing out harsh criticism to Lucilius and himself, but it must be remembered that it is no easy task to wake someone or one's own self from the slumber of habit and distraction and move them into action. This perhaps holds doubly true for the person new to recovery. To begin to pay attention to one's thoughts and emotions that have been anesthetized through years of alcoholic drinking is a Herculean task (see Chapter 6 for some inspiration from him). So how, practically speaking, can the recovering person heed Seneca's wake-up call in an AA context? Newcomers in meetings will begin hearing about morning meditation practices, which serve the function, among others we have discussed in earlier chapters, of awakening the reader to the present day, the twenty-four hours ahead.[5] Let us consider Pierre Hadot on Stoic spiritual practices side-by-side with Bill W.'s words from the "Big Book":

> First thing in the morning, we should go over in advance what we have to do during the day, and decide on the principles which will guide our actions.
>
> (*Philosophy as a Way of Life*, 85)

> On awakening let us think about the twenty-four hours ahead. We consider our plans for the day. Before we begin, we ask God to direct our thinking, especially asking that it be divorced from self-pity, dishonest or self-seeking motives. Under these conditions we can employ our mental faculties with assurance, for after all God gave us brains to use. Our thought-life will be placed on a much higher plane when our thinking is cleared of wrong motives.
>
> (*Alcoholics Anonymous,* 4th ed., 86)

These are but two of the myriad meditations of the type recovering people utilize each morning. Whatever specific form they take, the morning meditation generally provides answers to three essential questions: (1) What are you? (2) When are you? (3) What are you doing? The morning meditation first reminds us that we are alcoholics, the forgetting of which fact brings destructive and potentially deadly consequences. In the case of Bill's words quoted above, the fact that we are reading the words from a book entitled *Alcoholics Anonymous* helps to hammer home the point. Second, it slows us down, bringing us to the when we are, i.e., the present moment. This is crucial. Waking up and immediately plunging into a hectic day via racing to get ready for work with all that entails, the preparation of coffee and food, getting the kids ready, transportation arrangements, dressing and getting oneself presentable, etc., is to ensure that one lives in the same kind of chaotic frame of mind that is so familiar to the alcoholic. Living alcoholically meant placing a priority on something that actively interfered with everything else we wanted to do. The resultant chaos in our lives was completely unmanageable. We need to stop living in a way that psychologically and physiologically invokes feelings similar to that chaos. Recovery works on a cognitive behavioral therapy basis to change our thinking from scattered and chaotic to mindful and deliberate. The beginning of this process for many is when their sponsor first suggests that they start setting an alarm for ten, fifteen, or twenty minutes earlier than they would normally get up in order to provide a buffer of time between awakening and plunging into the day's tasks. This period is for meditation and rehearsal of the day. This period utilized well brings the mind's attention to this particular day rather than letting it drift toward the past, where shame and guilt dwell, or toward the future, where fear and anxiety make their abodes. Many AAs find themselves extending the period of time for meditation as they progress in recovery. The ten minutes earlier wake-up time can seem like a tall order early on, but many people with long-term recovery make sure to allot a full half hour or more to their meditation practice and never seem to miss the sleep. Most find it very beneficial to trade off that extra hour of television or similar distraction at night for an unhurried time for contemplation before the day begins.

Rehearsal of the tasks of the present given day often alleviates anxiety that tends to only accumulate with the rushing from one task to another. It also provides the opportunity to practice specific Stoic strategies such as *praemeditatio malorum* (see Chapter 2). If, for example, you have a meeting with the head of your company about your future there and you have reason to anticipate an offer of continued employment with a reasonable raise, it is very beneficial to remind yourself that you do not have all the information and it is possible that you could be walking into a meeting where you will be told your position is being phased out over the next three months. However remote a possibility this seems to you in your analysis, it is better to have already thought out how you would theoretically deal with it than to be left in the state the Greeks called *aporia*, or "resourcelessness," by the shock of the news.

At this juncture Seneca shifts his focus from how we lose time to how we fail to value time:

> Quem mihi dabis qui aliquod pretium tempori ponat, qui diem aestimet, qui intellegat se cotidie mori?
>
> Whom can you give to me who places the proper value on time, who gives an accurate estimate of the value of a day, who understands that he himself is dying on a daily basis?

Similar emphasis is placed on the present day in many recovery meditations. Consider the following from the Sanskrit poet Kalidasa, a poem quoted at the opening of Hazelden's Twenty-Four Hours a Day book of daily meditations:

> Look to this day, for it is life,
> The very life of life,
> In its brief course lie all the realities
> And verities of existence:
> The bliss of growth, the splendor of action,

The glory of power.
For yesterday is but a dream
And tomorrow is only a vision.
But today, well lived, makes every yesterday
A dream of happiness!
And every tomorrow a vision of hope.
Look well, therefore, to this day!

Valuing the present moment, the current day, is central to the AA philosophy of life. When the recovering person takes the step (pun intended) from "I don't have to drink, just for today" to "I don't have to live as I always have, just for today" or "I don't have to be who I was, just for today" they open a panorama on the changes possible in recovery beyond freedom from the enslaving substance. They also move toward the philosophical heart of the Stoic perspective on time Seneca wishes Lucilius and us to grasp.

The striking question Seneca formulates about the awareness of dying every day flips the perspective on daily living. Ancient Greek philosophy from the time of Socrates on had the habit of doing just this, reformulating the central question of eudaimonistic ethics from how to live well to how to die well. By focusing our attention on our day of birth as the first day we begin to die, the reality of our time and its end is pushed out of some imagined future into the present in an effort to awaken us to living this day with the conscious awareness that we are also dying this day. Such a perspective is not to be confused with either morbid reflection or some sort of "anything goes" because "you only live once" credo. Rather, it is intended as a corrective to default false perspectives on the nature of time and death and the attendant lack of ethical clarity.

> In hoc enim fallimur, quod mortem prospicimus: magna pars eius iam praeterit; quidquid aetatis retro est mors tenet.
>
> (*EM* 1.1.2)
>
> In this matter we are deceived, namely about the fact that we look at death as a future prospect. A great part of it has already passed by; whatever time is in the past death has hold of.

It might sound trite to us to say, "The past is dead and gone," but Seneca wishes us to see the true value of looking at the past as belonging to death. On the one hand, this perspective can help free us from the burden of carrying our past into the present (along the lines that several of the steps, especially Four, Eight, and Nine, aim to do). On the other hand, it reminds us to be awake to the life that does not belong to death, i.e., the now.

The other principal threat to living well in the present is, of course, dwelling mentally on the things to come. The only outcome can be anxiety, and since most alcoholics cite anxiety of one variety or another as part of why they loved and depended on the relief that alcohol offered, we can easily see how recovery must seek to offer healthy alleviation of anxiety. Anxiety is, according to Seneca in this letter, the product of a kind of hanging onto a tomorrow that isn't here:

> Fac ergo, mi Lucili, quod facere te scribis, omnes horas complectere; sic fiet ut minus ex crastino, si hodierno manum inieceris.

> Do, my Lucilius, that which you write that you are doing; embrace all hours; thus it will come out that you depend less on tomorrow, if you put your hand in to claim today.

Here we might further contemplate Seneca's message with his aphoristic formulation about expectation from a separate work:

> Expectatio, quod pendet ex crastino, perdit hodiernum.
>
> (*De Brevitate Vitae* 9.1)
>
> Expectation, because it depends on tomorrow, destroys today.

Recovery literature and AA meetings are filled with similar perspectives, with the particular form of the ethical wisdom ranging from the highbrow, such as the Sanskrit poem cited above; to the medium, such as "expectations are future resentments"; to the graphically lowbrow, such as "If you have one foot in yesterday and one in tomorrow, you are pissing all over today."

Seneca next asks Lucilius and us to contemplate both how time moves and our possession of it:

> Dum differtur vita transcurrit omnia, Lucili. Omnia, Lucili, aliena sunt, tempus tantum nostrum est; in huius rei unius fugacis ac lubricae possessionem natura nos misit, ex qua expellit quicumque vult.
>
> While time is deferred it runs by. All things are external to us, Lucilius; time alone is ours. Nature has sent us the possession of this one slippery, escaping thing, from which whoever wishes to evict us can.

The first emphasis here is on a commonplace of philosophical perspectives on time, probably best known by Vergil's famous *tempus fugit* formulation: *Sed fugit interea, fugit inreparabile tempus* ("Irreparable time runs away, but in the meantime it runs away") (*Georgics* III.284-5). The next thought calls us back to the heart of the first chapter of our journey here. By labeling all things as external or "not our own," Seneca evokes in the context of time the dichotomy central to Epictetus' ethics, that between what is up to us and what is not. In doing so, Seneca reminds us that the present is all we have and thus urges us to make wise use of it.

As we have seen, the wisdom of the meditations AAs utilize brings forth similar perspectives on time as Seneca in this letter. But AA has other ways in which it offers valuable philosophical perspectives on time. Many of these are part of the oral fabric of meetings. Old-timers in AA evoke in their own idiosyncratic fashion the possession of the present in contrast to the past, which does not belong to us. One might expect old-timers to be very emphatic about just how long they have been sober and exactly what that means (and they sometimes can be). But, quite strikingly, one of the things I have heard *exclusively* from old-timers in AA is the query, "What time did you get up this morning?" If the interlocutor responds with a time that is an hour earlier than the old-timer, they will say that "you have more sobriety than I do today." This is a powerful way to express the one-day-at-a-time AA philosophy. The old-timer is in effect saying that their thirty-four (or whatever number) years of sobriety are *aliena*—not their own possession, as the Romans Stoics label it, since they are past. This by no means negates the wisdom and experience acquired over those thirty-four years, but it does put the focus on today for the more recently sober person in much the same way as Seneca is doing for Lucilius in this letter.

Seneca wishes Lucilius and us next to contemplate the source of this one true possession of ours, namely nature. Seneca is assuredly utilizing *natura* here in the sense of the *ratio naturae*, the divine force that fashioned us as ephemeral creatures. As discussed at various earlier points in this book, the aim of alignment with the *ratio naturae* is for the Stoic analogous to the recovery person's alignment with their Higher Power. In both Stoicism and recovery, one of the first alignments required is getting in tune with living in the present. What Seneca is reminding us of is that living thusly is what we were designed for by our very nature. By dwelling on the past, either with regret or excessive nostalgia, or imagining and fantasizing about the future, we are in fact living *contra naturam* in the Stoic sense. Since Stoicism reiterates "follow nature" as one of its core precepts (discussed in depth in Chapter 4), we act least in accord with our own very nature when letting our minds stay too long in recollection of the past or future revelry.

The letter next turns to our penchant for valuing all the wrong things while being careless with our time:

> Et tanta stultitia mortalium est ut quae minima et vilissima sunt, certe reparabilia, imputari sibi cum impetravere patiantur, nemo se iudicet quicquam debere qui tempus accepit, cum interim hoc unum est quod ne gratus quidem potest reddere.

> And further the foolishness of mortals is so great that they allow whatever things are of least value and cheapest, and surely

> replaceable, when they have gained them, to be charged to their account; no one judges that he owes anything who has received our time, even though in the meantime this is the one thing which not even the grateful person is in fact able to return to us.

The choice of the adjective "replaceable" (*reparabilia*) here evokes the fundamental opposition between things that can be replaced and time, which cannot be, through Seneca's emphatic recall of Vergil's famous dictum about irreplaceable time (*inreparabile tempus*; see just above). Awareness of the present moment is a counterbalance to the human tendency to value the replaceable things and take for granted the irreplaceable ones.

Recovery literature places a great deal of emphasis on the awareness and appreciation of time, but it is in our relationships, particularly in our roles as sponsors and sponsees, where the time spent working with another alcoholic can really open our perspectives on the use of our time. In meaningful contrast to Seneca's general assessment of the lack of feeling of obligation on the part of those utilizing another's time, AAs learn early on that a great debt is owed for the use of their sponsor's and other trusted advisors' and friends' time. This debt can never be paid back to the one who gave it, as Seneca says, but it must be paid forward with the generous expenditure of one's own time working with newcomers in turn. All of this leads to one of AA's famous paradoxes: "You can only keep what you have by giving it away." So although a grateful alcoholic cannot give us back our time, we can know that our time freely given makes us grateful for the time that was given to us when we first began to work a program of recovery. This grateful awareness marks our time as meaningful in comparison with our years lost to the bottle.

Sponsees in early recovery are often eagle-eyed when it comes to how well their sponsors are practicing what they preach. Seneca is by no means oblivious to this fundamental aspect of the mentor–mentee relationship. In this instance, he chooses to formulate Lucilius' query about his practice of his preaching and answer it himself:

> Interrogabis fortasse quid ego faciam qui tibi ista praecipio. Fatebor ingenue: quod apud luxuriosam sed diligentem evenit, ratio mihi constat inpensae. Non possum dicere nihil perdere, sed quid perdam et quare et quemadmodum dicam; causas paupertatis meae reddam.
>
> You will perhaps ask how I, who gives these precepts to you, am doing. I will confess it openly: that which comes out amidst my indulgence and vigilance, my accounting of my expenditure is steady. I cannot claim that I have wasted nothing, but what I waste and why and how I can describe. I will give an account of my poverty.

Seneca's self-auditing here is a fundamental practice of both Stoicism and recovery. In AA parlance, Seneca's practice of examining the whats, whys, and hows of his spent time is part of a daily inventory, the equivalent of the ongoing inventory work of the Tenth Step, which is the small-scale day-at-a-time version of the inventory we did on our past in the Fourth Step. Perhaps not surprisingly, Bill W.'s choice of metaphorical language to illustrate the purpose and function of the Fourth Step inventory centers, like Seneca's, on business accounting:

> A business which takes no regular inventory usually goes broke. Taking a commercial inventory is a fact-finding and fact-facing process. It is an effort to discover the truth about the stock in trade.
>
> (*Alcoholics Anonymous*, 4th ed., 64)

Taking account of how one's time is spent is a critical part of beginning to value it more. For the alcoholic, wasted time is time spent in morbid self-reflection, fear of the future, self-pity, and similar emotional pitfalls to which the addict's mind, overly focused on the self, is so prone. But Seneca's message also contains a healthy perspective on one's efforts to better oneself, reminiscent of another famous AA motto: "Progress, not perfection." Seneca is not not wasting time, but he is on top of it, which is where mindfulness begins. And he is not beating himself up about his shortcomings, but rather honestly presenting his current situation with an eye to improvement. The recovering individual will recognize in Seneca a man who also finds himself in the range in which most of us who maintain a rewarding sobriety spend our time: we hope to do better but know we are not falling down on the job, either. There is vigilance and continuous effort.

Seneca's final accounting here leads him to a somewhat wistful yet ultimately hopeful perspective on time:

> Sed evenit mihi quod plerisque non suo vitio ad inopiam redactis: omnes ignoscunt, nemo succurrit. Quid ergo est? Non puto pauperem cui quantulumcumque superest sat est.
>
> It comes out for me as it does for most driven to poverty through no fault of their own: all pardon me, but none can help.

> What therefore can be done? I do not consider him poor for whom however little remains is sufficient.

Contentedness with what you have left and a willingness to use it well are Seneca's lessons. These are, of course, central spiritual teachings of recovery as well. The disease of alcoholism is often called the "disease of more." With the insatiable need for alcohol like a black hole at the center of their life, the alcoholic is more prone than most to an abiding sense of restless dissatisfaction. A focal point of recovery is the dwelling on the fact that we do in fact have "enough," however much that is. Gratitude lists help some realize this. Others find that the inside work of the steps aids them in reaching the realization that satisfaction never came with having more to begin with. Time is one of the more challenging ways in which the question of enough is front and center. After all, years (that the locust hath eaten) have been lost to the bottle, often along with the families, relationships, careers, hobbies, and more built and destroyed during those years. How can one respond to such a monumental loss? Only by realizing that whatever is left is enough, if lived well. And living well means living sober.

Having summarized his own inventory results, Seneca returns to the advisory mode of mentor:

> Tu tamen malo serves tua, et bono tempore incipies.
> All the same I prefer that you preserve your time, and you will begin in good time.

The principle of satisfaction with the time one has remaining does not prevent the older man from exhorting the younger to make use of his likely temporal good fortune. Within AA this principle often manifests itself in the approach of older AAs to those who found sobriety while still young. From the vantage of thousands of meetings, I can say anecdotally that most of the folks with long-term sobriety with whom I have had contact found sobriety in their late thirties or early forties. Certainly, some make it in their twenties and others in their sixties, but there is clearly a point of no return reached for the majority of alcoholics in the thirty-five to forty-five range when one either sobers up or finishes the job of drinking oneself to death. To appreciate the opportunity that a twenty-five-year-old sober person has could make a forty-five-year-old with five years in the program jealous, but this would be a sign of spiritual sickness. Like Seneca, the recovering individual who has made peace with time can both realize they had enough for themself and be happy for the opportunity that someone finding recovery very young has. At the same time, it adds heft to the older recovering person's advice to appreciate the opportunity afforded by finding AA sooner than most. As is frequently stated in a multitude of ways in meetings, one can never be sure that they have another recovery in them. The circumstances leading to the openness and willingness to fully invest in one's recovery often cannot be recreated for people afflicted with a disease that thrives off being closed off and recalcitrant. There is, in fact, a time that qualifies as too late, though one might never know when that is. Seneca closes his letter on a warning about just this, a too-late attempt at taking account of one's time:

> Nam ut visum est maioribus nostris, "sera parsimonia in fundo est"; non enim tantum minimum in imo sed pessimum remanet. Vale.

> For as it appeared to our ancestors, "thriftiness is too late when at the bottom of the barrel"; for in truth not only is it the least but also the worst which remains in the dregs. Farewell.

Seneca's advice here is equally applicable to getting sober and to living well in sobriety as we have seen throughout the letter. It may serve as a wake-up call to the decades-sober person who has become complacent and not made a good account of their time; or it may serve as a warning to the young person like Lucilius who makes the erroneous assumption that there will be plenty of time for recovery when they are older. Either way, today is the day. A reckoning with time cannot be put off.

By concluding his letter with a saying from the ancestors, Seneca places a double emphasis on the importance of his subject. Inventorying one's time is not just a Stoic practice, but a sensible response to the simple wisdom of the old Roman ways. Here at the close of this first letter Seneca again fuses the wisdom of Stoic philosophy with the *mos maiorum*, a topic we discussed in depth back in Chapter 3.

6

Philosophical Exemplars and Recovery Role Models

One of the most distinctive hallmarks of Roman intellectual life, one at the very heart of their way of thinking, is the ubiquitous and profound use of *exempla*, the fashioning of paradigms for virtuous behavior out of the heroes of the past who both illustrate and embody a particular virtue or perspective. Numerous figures might come to mind for those acquainted with Roman history, such as Horatius Cocles, who became an eternal model of self-sacrifice by holding off the enemy to let others cross the bridge to safety, and then cutting off his own means of escape by destroying the bridge so the enemy might not enter Rome, leaving himself on the wrong bank of the river. The Roman Stoics unsurprisingly also employ various *exempla* to illustrate what an individual on the Stoic path looks like and how they act.

Though Cato the Younger, a Stoic who died by suicide after losing the battle for liberty in fighting against the aims of Julius Caesar, became a prominent Stoic exemplar, it is the heroes of Greek myth whom the Stoics often preferred to utilize as paradigms.[1] Two of these ancient heroes predominate as *exempla* for the Roman Stoics, Heracles (Hercules in Latin) and Odysseus (Ulysses in Latin).[2] The unique appropriateness of these two figures as *exempla* for Stoic philosophers is twofold; firstly, each is renowned for endurance of suffering, and secondly, the labors of Heracles, and the obstacles to his homecoming that Odysseus faces, provide extremely rich mythic material for allegorical interpretation, a favorite pastime of the philosophers. Heracles' life is spent in the completion of near impossible tasks set for him by the vindictiveness of Hera; and Odysseus endures more in his struggle to return home than any other Greek. Many of the famous Twelve Labors of Heracles and the challenges Odysseus faced on his long homecoming were the subject of allegorical interpretation by ancient mythographers and remain employed in this fashion by modern psychologists and philosophers. In order to have a picture of the kind of interpretation involved here, let us consider just one example briefly. The psychologist Jonathan Shay in his excellent *Odysseus in America* shows how for a combat veteran like Odysseus trying to return to the civilian world, the lure of the Sirens has more to do with their recognition of his trauma than the temptation of seductress figures they often appear as in popular myth. The danger in moving toward them lies in moving toward one's earlier understanding of self as soldier with its warrior code culminating in a courageous death in battle rather than in moving toward a civilian life where survival itself is the victory. Like Odysseus, the combat veteran in therapy moves away from the allure of the warrior code toward a life that views survival as the priority. Modern psychotherapy informed by cognitive behavioral terminology terms the process of contemplating how Odysseus handled the danger of the Sirens "modeling."[3] So again, a modern psychological interpretation echoes ancient Stoic practice. The Stoics deeply believed in the value of "modeling" heroes in both general and specific scenarios.

In this chapter we will look at how the Roman Stoics employed Heracles and Odysseus as models of Stoic ethical values and perspectives. Then we will consider how recovering individuals can similarly make proper use of models, both in the interpretative mode of the Stoics and in the use of their very own recovery models, including sponsors, spiritual mentors, and old-timers who help guide them on their path. But first we need to look at an exemplary use of Heracles that predates the Stoics to see how a mythic hero was first transformed into an ethical one.

Heracles (Hercules)

Heracles as General Exemplar

Heracles was *the* exemplar, prior to becoming the specifically Stoic one, associated with the philosophical choice between virtue and vice thanks to a famous passage from Xenophon's (*c.* 430–355 BCE) *Memorabilia* (2.1.21–34) where Socrates relates Prodicus' allegorical tale of Heracles' choice of virtue over vice. This charming and enlightening tale shows us one of the ways in which myth was transmuted into philosophy:

They say that Heracles, when he was moving from boyhood into adolescence, at which time the young are becoming in command of themselves and show whether they will turn along the path of excellence in life or the path of baseness, came out into a restful spot and sat puzzling over which of the two paths he would turn upon.

Two women appeared to him in that spot and, both tall, approached him. The one woman was comely to look upon and naturally free; her body ornamented with purity, her eyes with modesty, and her bearing with self-control, and her clothing was white.

But the other woman was nourished beyond the necessary to the point of softness, and her complexion was made up so that it would seem to appear whiter and rosier than it in fact was, and her bearing was such that it would appear more erect than it naturally was. She held her eyes open and her clothing was that by which her youthful bloom might especially shine forth. She looked at herself frequently, then looked to see whether anyone else was looking at her, and repeatedly glanced at her own shadow.

When they came closer to Heracles, the first woman spoken of came forward in an even manner, but the other, wanting to outstrip the first, ran up to Heracles and said to him: "I see, Heracles, that you are puzzling over what road you should turn down in life. If you make me your friend, I will lead on the pleasantest and easiest path, and you will be deprived of the taste of none of the pleasures of life and you will live a life unacquainted with hardships. For, first off, you will take thought of neither wars nor business affairs, but rather you will spend your day looking into what food and drink you might find most enjoyable, or what you might most delight in seeing or hearing, or in what scents and touches you might feel pleasure, or with what darlings you might be especially happy spending your time, or how you might sleep most softly, and how you might obtain all these things with the very least effort.

But if ever there is suspicion regarding scarcity about where all these pleasures will come from, have no fear that I might lead you to acquiring these things from the toil and suffering of your body and soul, but rather others will work for them and you will enjoy them, keeping away from nothing which is able to supply some profit. For I offer to those who associate with me the capability of gaining advantage in every situation."

Heracles, having heard these things, said "Woman, what is your name?" And she responded, "Those dear to me call me Happiness, but those who loathe me, giving me a nickname, call me Baseness."

And then the other woman having approached him said, "I also am come to you, Heracles, knowing your parents and having observed closely your nature during your education. From which I am hopeful that, if you should turn your path toward me, you would surely become a doer of noble and august deeds, and I will be more honored and shine more remarkably because of your good deeds. I will not deceive you with preludes of pleasure, but I will explain how things truly are and in what way the gods have set them up. The gods have given to man nothing of all good and noble things without toil and practice. But if you wish the gods to be propitious toward you, it is necessary to honor them; if you wish to be loved by friends, it is necessary to do good deeds for them; if you are eager to be honored by some city, it is necessary

> to do something beneficial for the city; if you deem it worthy to be marveled at by all of Greece, it is necessary to try to do well for Greece; and if you wish the land to bear fruit unbegrudgingly, it is necessary to take care of the land; and if you deem it right to become rich in flocks, it is necessary to tend those flocks; and if you have the impulse to grow great through war and to be able to liberate friends and subdue enemies, it is necessary to learn the arts of war from those knowledgeable in them and to practice how it is appropriate to use them; and if you want to have power in your body, it is necessary to habituate the body to serve the mind and train it with toil and sweat." And Baseness, making answer, said, as Prodicus tells us, "Are you considering how rugged and long is that road which this woman lays out for you? But I will lead you by an easy and short road to happiness."[4]

In these final lines we have the juxtaposition of the two paths with Heracles in a quandary over which to follow, or "Hercules at the Crossroads," a scene rendered in a variety of ways by numerous Renaissance painters. The change from the mythical impetus for the hard road he travels, Hera's enmity, to an actual choice of his own in pursuit of virtue is critical. The path of philosophy must be chosen; it cannot be forced upon anyone.

Heracles' choice and the language of Xenophon's description of it may quickly call to mind for members of Alcoholics Anonymous one of the most well-known sections of the "Big Book." It is so well-known because the reading of this passage is the way most meetings officially begin. The reading is from "How It Works," the beginning of chapter 5 of the "Big Book," where it quite literally lays out "the path" that AAs follow:

> Our stories disclose in a general way what we used to be like, what happened, and what we are like now. If you have decided you want what we have and are willing to go to any length to get it—then you are ready to take certain steps. At some of these we balked. We thought we could find an easier, softer way. But we could not. With all the earnestness at our command, we beg of you to be fearless and thorough from the very start. Some of us have tried to hold on to our old ideas and the result was nil until we let go absolutely.
> (*Alcoholics Anonymous*, 4th ed., 58)

It is striking how similarly the path of virtue in Greek philosophy is portrayed to the path of recovery in AA. The easier, softer way is a trick. The road of virtue and likewise that of recovery is narrow, steep, and rugged. It is not for the faint of heart. It requires fearlessness and is the hard rather than the easy path. It does not in the least resemble the easiest and pleasantest road that Vice offers to Heracles. An overwhelming majority will not make it. But we have exemplars to follow: Heracles in philosophy, Bill and Dr. Bob in AA, and all the people we encounter in life and in AA who trod a path of life that was challenging but well-lived. For me personally, I also have a moment I cherish from early in my recovery when an old-timer, a giant of a man at six feet seven inches and over 300 pounds, pulled me aside at the close of a meeting and, taking my hand in his own bear-sized paw, told me there was good news and bad news: "The bad news is that it is always uphill; the good news is that our legs get stronger." Heracles also grew stronger by taking the steep and rugged path.

Heracles as Specifically Stoic Exemplar: Attitude, Character Formation, and Service

The early use of Heracles as a general exemplar of philosophical virtue gives us a kind of macroscopic view of the mythic hero as incarnation of ethical beacon. In what follows we will examine at the microscopic level uses by the Roman Stoics of Heracles as exemplar of specific psychological attitudes and virtuous dispositions.

First let us loop back to Chapter 1 and the philosophical athlete of Epictetus. As the reader may recall, Heracles was the exemplary athlete since the proper name for his famous Twelve Tasks is *athloi* in Greek, whence the word *athlete* in English, "labors" being a Latin translation. Epictetus repeatedly employs the figure of Heracles as the embodiment of his particular approach to Stoicism. Here, for example, Epictetus brings Heracles forward as an example of the right kind of attitude to cultivate toward life's challenges:

> But Heracles, when he was being exercised by Eurystheus, did not think himself miserable but completed all the tasks commanded to him without hesitation. Was this man being trained and exercised by Zeus about to whine and complain?
>
> (*Discourses* 3.22.57)

Epictetus here makes his point more emphatic through a word play in the Greek. The word for "miserable" is *athlios* and the word for "being trained" is *athloumenos*. And so Epictetus asks how any athlete could be miserable when he is being trained to be better? The *athlos* is thus he who is never *athlios* because his attitude to all of life's challenges is to embrace them as training obstacles. And Heracles is the paradigmatic athlete.[5] As we explored in Chapter 2, attitude and perspective are within our power, while our circumstances are not. This, as discussed earlier, is the foundational Stoic idea behind cognitive behavioral therapy. In a very similar vein is Epictetus' employment of Heracles at *Discourses* 1.6.33:

> Or what do you think he would have amounted to, if there had not been a lion like the one which he encountered or a hydra, and a stag, and a boar, and wicked and brutal men, whom he made it his business to drive out and clear away?

Here we see how Epictetus points us toward two central aspects of Heracles' labors: firstly, what kind of man they made him become; and secondly, what service his actions in performing them provided to the rest of humankind.

Recovery is not simply like the path of virtue in the general sense that it is a narrow, rugged, and hard road. AA really emphasizes the change in the person brought about by their journey on the hard road. Consider how the excerpt from "How It Works" quoted above juxtaposes the individual pre- and post-recovery: "what we used to be like … and what we are like now." As recovery literature and recovering people constantly emphasize, the path of recovery is not only about not drinking but also, and perhaps even more so, about changing how one thinks and approaches the world. One of the most fundamental and foundational of the personality shifts is from the typical addict's deeply ingrained self-centeredness to a service-focused mentality. This change is adduced by many an alcoholic as the saving grace of their newfound lives in recovery. Becoming interested in service to others begins with a willingness to help fellow travelers on the recovery path through service in meetings and/or in the AA superstructure, on speaking commitments, and as a sponsor. But perhaps the most profound change comes with a new perspective on our work outside of AA.

Using my own experience here, I can reflect on the changes in my relationship with my career in teaching. I have always loved teaching. I have great enthusiasm for the content I teach, and I enjoy the moments of recognition and breakthrough seen in students. I think I excel at it; and have been told so by others in a variety of ways. But though I could see what I was offering to the individual student and a whole class as intellectually valuable, I never conceived of teaching as a service activity until I was in recovery. I began to see that my job was also a means of giving back, not just doing what I loved and was good at. Becoming aware of this dimension, I have sought to incorporate it into my approach as well. I have heard many a fellow AA share similar stories about how their relationship toward their work changed in recovery and a service-oriented perspective began to influence both their approach and attitude. Alternatively, not a few have come to see their work as not being service-oriented and this has led, along with other considerations, naturally, to a career change in recovery. Service to all humankind can take on many forms, of course, and to those not familiar with AA, a conversation between two recovering individuals in which one mentions feeling good because they had received a call from an acquaintance who was in need of a ride because it provided them an opportunity to be of service that day can come across as bizarre in a world where many would focus on the inconvenience to their own schedules of the request.

In a similar vein, Epictetus would have us contemplate Heracles' labors. They changed him as a person, and the focus of these labors shifted from the standard mythical heroic archetype centered on the strength of the hero and what it allowed him to overcome as an individual to the service he was performing for all humankind. Note how Epictetus moves away from the mythical animals to the wicked and brutal men Heracles drove away to make the world safe for everyone else in his reflection on the labors quoted above.

We might be inclined at this juncture to ask why we need to contemplate such great challenges as represented by the deeds of a Heracles in order to bring about a change in ourselves. Epictetus anticipates such a question and has an answer for us as well:

> But you are no Heracles, you say, and you cannot clear away the wickedness of other men, nay, nor are you even a Theseus, to clear away the ills of Attica merely. Very well, clear away your own then.

Epictetus here makes clear to us that modeling does not mean aiming to accomplish deeds similar to those of Heracles or Theseus—or, for that matter, any heroic figure. It means we take the same mental and philosophical approach to our own difficulties and evils as they did to theirs. "Clear away your own" matches the third part of the AA mantra, "Trust God. Help others. And clean house!" Here we begin to verge toward allegorical interpretation as Epictetus continues:

> From just here, from out of your own mind, cast not Procrustes and Sciron,[6] but grief, fear, desire, envy, joy at others' ills; cast out greed, effeminacy, incontinency.

Epictetus now reveals our personal equivalents to the labors of Heracles. The labors are a model for our approach to our psychological work on ourselves in pursuit of serenity and happiness. Coincidently, there are Twelve Steps with which to undertake these labors toward psychological and spiritual health, just as there are Twelve Labors that Heracles must complete. The Twelve Steps of AA address in detail the sources of emotional turmoil cited by Epictetus. It is no wonder, then, that many folks with long-term sobriety speak in meetings not of their sobriety, but of their emotional sobriety. The issue of drink evaporates for most sometime within the first year of recovery, but the Heraclean challenge of dealing with Epictetus' litany of emotional upsets quoted above for a person who is as maladapted to "living life on life's terms," as most addicts tend to be, is a lifelong journey in seeking tranquility and peace of mind.

It isn't difficult to imagine an objection to this model of happiness. How is continuous wrestling with challenges the path to peace of mind? While it might sound paradoxical to some, to AAs it is easy to point to their thinking while physically sober but devoid of the steps, meditation, and meetings. The default psychological setting of the addict is a state of "dis-ease," an experience of feeling "restless, irritable, and discontent."[7] Many alcoholics and addicts have found that the true nature of their "dis-ease" isn't obvious to them until the alcohol and/or drugs have been removed from the equation. It is then that they are confronted with the fact that alcohol was not the problem, but the solution turned destroyer. So it is that there is little long-term sense of serenity found in simply eliminating the negative consequences arising from addiction. The absence of police involvement, legal fees, broken relationships, empty bank accounts, terrible hangovers, and withdrawals, etc., that usually follow abstinence are very, very nice benefits, but this lack of troubles does not constitute a way of life. The Stoics would seem to agree with those in recovery that real happiness could not be adequately defined as an absence of troubles. Becker, a neo-Stoic whose work we encountered in the discussion of agency in Chapter 1, is helpful here. When he seeks to convey what constitutes Stoic happiness, one definition he utilizes reads as follows: "an impressive array of developed endowments and constructed traits operating in a challenging environment."[8] Again, to many, this might not accord with their intuition about "happiness." Perhaps for some freedom from care, a sunny day, and a book on the beach really do count as happiness. But the addict in recovery will recognize Becker's definition as markedly similar to the serenity obtained by the employment of the aforementioned "toolbox" of "spiritual tools" that allows them to correct their default thinking, rife as it is with all the sources of emotional turmoil Epictetus cited as the real antagonists of the Stoic. Utilizing a set of spiritual tools in order to live a physically sober and emotionally sober life is happiness. As the full version of the "Serenity Prayer" puts it, people in recovery make it a habit of "accepting hardship as a pathway to peace."[9]

The Shared Exemplarity of Heracles and Odysseus

Cosmopolitanism

The Hellenistic philosophers are justly credited with the development of a perspective on citizenship that has its roots in both Socrates and the so-called "crazy Socrates," Diogenes the Cynic. These two earlier figures took a philosophical view toward the idea of where they were from and where they belonged that was antithetical to the prevailing historical attitudes that emphasized a person's connection to their city-state or *polis*. Hence the idea of cosmopolitanism was born, a move away from defining oneself as a citizen of Athens or Sparta or Thebes toward defining oneself as literally a citizen of the *cosmos*, or the universe. A close look at what this shift in perspective accomplishes ethically, and how Heracles and Odysseus are both stellar exemplars of it for Epictetus, provides some insights on the idea of "home" that share an important affinity with a view of "home" held in the world of recovery.

Epictetus cites Odysseus and Heracles together as his paradigms of cosmopolitanism:

> And man, in addition to being by nature high-minded and capable of desiring all the things that are outside his moral purpose, has this further quality, that, namely, of not being rooted nor growing in the earth, but of moving now to one place and now to another, at one time under the pressure of certain needs, and at another merely for the sake of spectacle. Now it was something of this sort

> which fell to the lot of Odysseus: "Many the men whose towns he beheld, and he learned of their temper."[10] And even before his time it was the fortune of Heracles to traverse the entire inhabited world; "Seeing the wanton behavior of men and the lawful,"[11] casting forth the one and the clearing the world of it, and introducing the other in its place.[12]

The real point, of course, is not that Odysseus and Heracles both wandered all over the place. It is what they got out of it, how it changed them. After detailing the friends and relationships Odysseus formed in all the other places he visited, Epictetus concludes with this reflection: "Wherefore he [i.e., Odysseus] had the power of living happily everywhere."[13]

As Heracles and Odysseus learned that everywhere could be a home to the man of cosmopolitan perspective, so AAs learn that meetings anywhere can serve as homes away from home. Many an AA member enjoys sharing exactly how and where they first found this to be true; and how invigorating it was. And many are quick to note that a meeting, wherever it is (even in the virtual rooms of Zoom post-COVID), is their truest home. We in recovery are citizens of a unique universal *polis* and this citizenship transcends not only geographical differences but also socioeconomic, ethnic, religious, and meteorological ones. The utter meaninglessness of such distinctions in the face of the one true life-or-death identity as alcoholic is a theme for Bill in his own reflections on things that can potentially stand in the way of recovery:

> In the beginning, it was four whole years before A.A. brought permanent sobriety to even one alcoholic woman. Like the "high

> bottoms", the women said they were different; ... The Skid-Rower said he was different ... so did the artists and professional people, the rich, the poor, the religious, the agnostic, the Indians and the Eskimos, the veterans, and the prisoners ... nowadays all of these, and legions more, soberly talk about how very much alike all of us alcoholics are when we admit that the chips are finally down.[14]

The primacy of the identity of the recovering individual is most fully realized when outside of one's accustomed surroundings. To be a world citizen for the Stoics and to be a recovering person both put the focus squarely on the universally shared conditions of life. The result is a sense of belonging. Feeling at home and not alone while traveling is a special element for the addict, one of whose psychological hallmarks is feeling alone and isolated even among loving friends and family. The cosmic home each AA member carries within them is brought to life in meetings in other cities and countries. This is very much akin to the Stoic view. As reason is the defining trait that transcends all other distinctions for them, so the shared suffering from the disease of alcoholism and the compassion for it found around the world turns the recovering person philosophically cosmopolitan.

This new way of looking at the place we call home is also the flip side of an old way of thinking when we were still drinking. Bill himself writes about the nature of the "geographic cure" that alcoholics still on the bottle futilely turn to in the hope that a change of scenery might straighten out their drinking. As alcoholics, we thought that a change in the circumstances around us, like moving from a cold and gray northern city to a bright beach town, would make the difference. It didn't. As people in recovery, we now know that there is an unchanging place within us that renders the geography surrounding us a minor concern. The geographical cure failed us in our addiction because, as the saying goes, "We take ourselves with us wherever we go." In the days of our addiction, this meant that our disease traveled within us and turned the bright beach town into as bleak a landscape as the cold and gray northern city we had fled. In recovery "we take ourselves with us" means that we have a core of selfhood rooted in the awareness of ourselves as alcoholics that cannot be taken from us by circumstances. Many recovering individuals first tap into this new selfhood in settings where alcohol is being served. Most agree that steering clear of places where alcohol is present is the best idea for newcomers. But as our sense of a recovering self grows, this is less and less of an issue. Bars, wedding receptions, sporting events, and the like that may have been territory sprinkled with landmines at one point become indistinguishable from places and events where there is no alcohol. Bill says the following about the alcoholic who has reached this entirely neutral attitude to alcohol:

> We are not fighting it, neither are we avoiding temptation. We feel as though we had been placed in a position of neutrality—safe and protected. We have not even sworn off. Instead, the problem has been removed. It does not exist for us.
>
> (*Alcoholics Anonymous*, 4th ed., 85)

Stoic *Oikeiosis*

The Stoic conception of cosmopolitanism ensures that we don't constrain our identity by our geographical circumstance in a way that matches how AA provides addicts with a "wherever you are, you are home" sense of belonging. Cosmopolitanism itself is an outgrowth of the Stoic concept of *oikeiosis*, the affinity and sense of appropriateness creatures feel for that which is particularly their own. Contemplating what makes an eagle an eagle, for example, we would think of its swiftness in descending on prey, its keen vision, and its particular means of grasping its prey, whence arises the name raptor—"snatcher" in Latin—for all birds of prey. For a human being, one clearly distinguishing affinity we possess in biological terms is walking upright. We are not born with the capability but grow into it as our own. The Stoics posited that there are affinities we possess as appropriate to the growth of our reasoning faculty in just the same way that learning to walk upright is appropriate to our physical growth. We may not be very kind and selfless as children, since our rationality is undeveloped; and we do not understand our appropriate role as rational creatures in a society of other rational creatures. If our rationality is unimpeded by overwhelming passions for power, wealth, glory, sexual conquest, and other similar pursuits that might render us particularly selfish, we will begin to see every other rational being as part of the same universe and deserving of our beneficence. For the Stoic, then, kindness is part of the *oikeiosis* of the rational animal, an integral part for which we have a natural affinity.

Epictetus provides us with a thoughtful reflection on kindness and our affinity for it. In doing so he clearly demonstrates that the use of *exempla* is in part about properly reading our examples. He wants us to be wary lest we fall into the trap of thinking in terms of the actual deeds or feats of popular Stoic exemplars of virtue. We are not meant to go strangling lions as Heracles did or holding our naked bodies against freezing marble in order to inure ourselves to the cold as Diogenes reportedly did. But Epictetus is out to show us more than the foolishness of over-literal emulation of models. He also makes uses of Heracles, and Diogenes as well, as antiparadigms, men whose exceptionalism can help us focus on our more banal exercise of virtue. And the banal exercise of virtue for him here encompasses the kindness and faithfulness that allow human beings to live together well. In an example that could be drawn straight from an AA meeting, Epictetus considers the situation of a man upset because his neighbor has thrown stones (they are literal here, but the metaphorical implications are clear enough). It is when a man responds to this kind of situation with kindness that he displays what is natural to a man. Retaliation would be natural for a wolf, but not for a man. At the end of a list of animals and their natural faculties the deprivation of which qualifies as the loss of their particular virtue, Epictetus frames his rhetorical question thus:

> And a dog? Is it when he can't fly? No, but when he can't keep the scent. Does it not follow then, that on the same principles a man is wretched, not when he is unable to choke lions, or throw his arms about statues (for no man has brought with him from nature into this world faculties for this), but when he has lost kindness and faithfulness?
>
> (*Discourses* 4.5.14)

It is not Heraclean strength or Diogenean physical endurance of suffering that is needed for living well, according to Epictetus, but rather a way to deal with resentment and anger. If we cannot keep these in check, we are at risk of losing that which defines our kind.

In AA the recovering individual assesses their emotional sobriety as the exercise of their virtue by much the same standard. Anger and resentment are, as discussed back in Chapter 2, viewed as the greatest dangers to the serenity and tranquility at the heart of the recovery lifestyle. These two emotions are particularly baleful branches of the addiction tree of which the trunk is our selfishness. Bill W. is very emphatic on this point:

> Whatever our protestations, are not most of us concerned with ourselves, our resentments, or our self-pity? Selfishness—self-centeredness! That, we think, is the root of our troubles. Driven by a hundred forms of fear, self-delusion, self-seeking, and self-pity, we step on the toes of our fellows and they retaliate. Sometimes they hurt us, seemingly without provocation, but we invariably find that at some time in the past we have made decisions based on self which later placed us in a position to be hurt.
>
> (*Alcoholics Anonymous*, 4th ed., 62)

We must call ourselves onto the carpet in our Tenth Step inventory if we find we have failed in this regard today. Perhaps no one hurled stones directly at my house today, but someone may well have cut me off in traffic or just been driving along at the speed limit when I thought it much more reasonable to do twenty miles an hour over it. Did I speed up and give them the bird? Did I pound the steering wheel and honk my horn an extra-long beat? These everyday situations are opportunities for us in recovery to gauge where we are emotionally. And the Stoics are with us, not asking that we try Diogenes' bizarre experiment in endurance of the cold, however much it might be calling out for a cinematic montage in "training to be a Cynic philosopher." After all, unless we are headed out on a mountaineering adventure to some snow-capped peak, being able to pause and remember that our kindness is a mark of who we are as human beings is likely to come in handier than a superhuman tolerance of freezing conditions.

Kindness is part of human *oikeiosis*, as is the cosmopolitan perspective. But these are just branches of the tree of *oikeiosis*. The root lies in what is most fundamental to the human animal, the ability to form judgments. Epictetus chooses an episode of Homer in which Odysseus has been stripped of all human accoutrements and is most animal-like to give us a Stoic reading of the scene that holds Odysseus up as an exemplar of that which truly belongs to every human being. Having washed up on the shore of the Phaeacians and utterly exhausted by his near drowning, he beds down under the cover of an olive tree. When he moves in the morning toward the voices of some young women, he is a pitiable wreck of man, clad only in the leaves he could scrounge together and wearing all the marks of his arduous journey. Homer compares him to a mountain lion who, driven by starvation, desperately leaves her mountain haunts in search of food down on the plains. In this animal-like state, Odysseus knows what is his own as a human being. Epictetus interprets the shame-inducing act of begging for food from strangers as the reliance of man on his own ability to judge what is and isn't up to him, an ability that man possesses an affinity for to match the affinity of the mountain lion's strength in hunting. Quoting Homer's description of Odysseus' move out of the trees onto the shore "as a lion reared in the mountains," Epictetus asks:

> In what did he trust? Not in reputation, or money, or office, but in his own might, that means, his judgments about the things which are under our control, and those which are not under our control.
>
> (*Discourses* III.XXVI.34–5, quoting from *Odyssey* Book VI.130)

Oikeiosis vis-à-vis Cosmopolitanism

In the examples discussed thus far, we have seen how both the cosmopolitan perspective of the Stoics and their doctrine of *oikeiosis* point to the universality of our identity as human beings in much the same way recovery emphasizes the universality of our identity as alcoholics and addicts. Yet there is nuance to the application of Stoic *oikeiosis* that explains preferences and their role in our lives and recovery. While Odysseus is exemplary in being able to be at home anywhere, he is also exemplary for the particular affinity he has with his craggy rock of an island home, Ithaca. Seneca makes use of this Odyssean exemplarity:

> Ulysses had thus hurried to the rocks of his own Ithaca, in the same way as Agamemnon did to the mighty walls of Mycenae. Indeed no one loves his fatherland because it is great, but because it is his own.
>
> (*Epistulae Morales* 66.26)[15]

As the rocky ground of Ithaca symbolically matches the tough and enduring Odysseus, so the noble walls suit Agamemnon's regal authority. This is not paradoxical to Stoic cosmopolitanism, but rather a lesson in acceptance of what place most befits our character, and, *ceteris paribus*, where we would *choose* to be most of the time. While the Stoic has a home everywhere other rational creatures are, they may also have a specific home that matches their personality.

Much the same is true of recovery. While the sense of being at home in any meeting provides the AA member with a powerful feeling of identification and connectedness, most people with long-term recovery also have a "Home Group," one particular meeting that they rarely miss attending and where they have shared in the ups and downs of recovery with a core group of regulars who also have this meeting as their "Home Group." In selecting a particular group to be one's home base, it is critical to consider what suits you and your character. As the tough, enduring sailor Odysseus loved his rocky, weather-beaten home, so the group one chooses ought to match one's personality. Some AAs love a "strict" meeting format, where only conference-approved literature (i.e., the "Big Book," *The Twelve and Twelve*, *As Bill Sees It*, etc.) is utilized for group reading and discussion. For others, a good fit might mean a looser meeting, where drugs other than alcohol are freely discussed and reading from nonconference-approved literature is common (i.e., Hazelden meditation books). For smokers, congregating outside for the "meeting before the meeting" and "the meeting after the meeting" might offer a higher level of fellowship. As long as the differences are about preferences and not an issue of core identification as an alcoholic, the choice we make is in keeping with both the AA and Stoic perspectives. However, if a high-bottom alcoholic from an upper-crust background fails to feel at home in a meeting with ex-cons and bikers, this could signify a failure of possessing the true universal identification as alcoholic that matches with Stoic cosmopolitanism.

Conclusion

Every individual's experience of recovery is unique, but there are some generally recognized phases with associated time frames as well as common patterns of growth and psychological development. The structure of this book is intended to mirror some of these. In reviewing, summarizing, and putting into the context of recovery the Stoic texts and ideas we have closely examined here, I think it important to keep in mind these phases and patterns of recovery that operate to create a true sea change in the individual. Such a total alteration of character is the ongoing effect of living by recovery principles, day by day, for years. As an old-timer told me when I was a newcomer, "There are only three things that you need to do: don't drink, go to meetings, and *change everything*." Epictetus made the same idea clear to those who attended his seminars. When explaining why he called his school "the hospital," he told them that when they departed after his lectures they would feel as if their very bones had been reset. So, here in the concluding portion of our journey with the Stoics I want to elucidate how my own bones were reset, as it were, according to general phase of recovery and corresponding Stoic teaching. I do not feel it out of place here to detail these changes through the lens of my own personal recovery journey since the power of identification with the person sharing is recognized as one of the keys to the efficacy of any program of recovery; and additionally because it is easy enough to extrapolate to a more general perspective on the changes I have experienced.

As I write this, I am just a few days removed from having picked up a coin for my eleventh anniversary of continuous sobriety. Reflecting back, I am still able to fully recognize the person I used to be, though I do not feel that I inhabit the same brain or body as him. What I mean by this is that I understand to a large degree who I was before sobriety, what motivated me, how I reacted to life, what I valued, etc., but I do not any longer think or feel as he did. My brain has been rewired through the combination of the *askesis*, that sum greater than its parts of discipline, practice, training, and habit, which we examined in Chapter 1, and the program of Alcoholics Anonymous. If I find myself becoming lax about the *askesis* and my involvement in AA, however, I begin to feel the creeping return of his thought patterns and must take action sooner rather than later. Chapter 1 is thus the chapter of this book most directly related to early recovery in that its establishment of disciplined practices and habits of mind corresponds to routinizing meeting attendance, meditation, inventory work, and one-on-one interaction with another recovering alcoholic, all aspects of recovery emphasized as essential for the newcomer to embrace. For the person further along in recovery, Chapter 1 provides philosophically driven insight on the generation of internal compulsion, that force that overcomes default excuses and laziness, which helps one continue to grow in life. This is the force that leads to the completion of the planned workout that was almost skipped due to it being a cold morning and the bed being comfortable and warm, the meeting attended that almost wasn't because there was something good debuting on Netflix, the new sponsee taken on in spite of the fact that working with him would eliminate the slot on Sundays for relaxing by doing nothing.

My emotional experience now consists of (mostly) responsive rather than reactive expression, often (but certainly not always) with a detached and objective (as possible) view of what I feel as I am feeling it. This is an entirely different emotional perspective than the one found in the me of eleven years ago. This fundamental change corresponds to an emotional fluency learned through the program of AA and the *armamentarium* of psychological tools discussed in Chapter 2. Learning a new fluency with emotions was for me a challenge that really began in earnest in my second year of sobriety. In exploring techniques for regulating our emotions we saw in Chapter 2 how the moral psychology of the Stoics dovetails with Cognitive Behavioral Therapy and learned the vocabulary and concepts of modern therapy and AA that map onto the Stoic spiritual practices.

Both mind and body seek a satisfied serenity today brought about by the fulfillment of meaningful and purposeful activities including teaching, exercise, hiking with friends, reading novels, and recovery work and play with fellow members of Alcoholics Anonymous. The wish to be engaged in these activities has replaced a bodily and mental demand for the feeling of numb oblivion my alcoholic self continuously sought. The imagistic language and metaphors we explored in Chapters 3 and 4 help conceptualize the individual purposeful actions within a comprehensive picture focused on the attainment and maintenance of a serene state of mind. Following Seneca's detailed philosophical painting can help us to contemplate our own lives as paintings on the easel in front of the palette, where a center of calm serenity exists whatever else is going on the picture.

A sense of connectedness gradually replaced the lonely arrogance that dominated my attitude toward the world. In AA I have learned to both give and receive help, something my active alcoholic self was exceptionally poor at doing. The connectedness and the sharing found in the rooms of AA helped lead me on a quest for what, other than fellow alcoholics, I felt spiritually connected to. My answer was found out in nature; and a new hobby of hiking led me to a naturalistic Higher Power as portrayed in the meditative texts of Marcus Aurelius and the *Tao Te Ching* in Chapter 4. The metaphors of the Roman philosopher-emperor and of Laozi guided me on the path of the deep contemplation of the natural world as a source of understanding and comfort.

My thoughts, most often in my alcoholism dwelling in morbid nostalgia with occasional jumps ahead to unrealistic fantasies of the future, find themselves more and more centered on today and its possibilities. Stoic mindfulness along with the continual insistence on the present as our only possession have aided me in moving away from my default nostalgia-focused thinking. We saw these perspectives put home in the form of a letter by Seneca that we approached as a meditation reading on the nature of time in Chapter 5. Truly embracing the one-day-at-a-time perspective of recovery not only in relation to remaining sober but other aspects of life as well is aided by reflection on Seneca's exhortation to truly account for and make good use of one's time.

I have learned how to observe closely people in and out of recovery who have qualities about them that I would like to possess, ranging from a calm demeanor in the face of great challenges to the way in which they approach their lives as creative endeavors. I have modeled myself on them, just as we saw in Chapter 6 the Stoics advise us to make use of Heracles and Odysseus as models for overcoming obstacles, enduring trials, knowing what is suitable for ourselves, and viewing ourselves as citizens of a world of recovery. Here we returned to the connection between the Stoics and Cognitive Behavioral Therapy to examine in detail how modeling works.

Perhaps the greatest concrete piece of evidence I have for the psychological and spiritual changes discussed above is this book itself. It required of me many things I only learned in recovery and philosophically internalized with my Stoic practices. I was an "if I can't do it alone, I don't want to do it" type. My lonely arrogance would have prevented me from admitting that I didn't even know where to get started in seeking a publisher for the type of book I had in mind, and which you are currently reading. I needed a great deal of guidance and support for this project to come together, as I had only ever published articles in academic journals or a book chapter in an academic text. I had to ask for help from people who knew the world of publishing. The academic articles were part of my career in a narrow sense; and they were do-it-myself projects, for the most part. Certainly, these articles dealt with things I care deeply about, but having them published was principally part of the job of being a professor. This book was conceived in a wholly different spirit of seeking connection, and through that connection, helping others.

Furthermore, this book would not have been possible for my rather close-minded, alcoholic Classicist self. It was only in the newly freed, recovering mind that open spiritual exploration took on a more serious role in my life, one that was not only about reading and studying different traditions, but actually implementing ethical wisdom from across the world in my daily life. Thus it was that deeper explorations in Buddhism and Taoism enriched my Stoic foundation and made me aware that others before me had hybridized Twelve-Step recovery with ancient philosophical perspectives in ways I found compelling and inspiring. As I have heard it put in various guises over the years, the alcoholic is wise to employ every available tool against the spiritual death that could lead to relapse. This panoplied approach to arming ourselves spiritually as recovering addicts is one that cherishes reading from and studying different spiritual traditions from the one that, by reason of childhood experience, education, personal preference, etc., we have at the center of our recovery. If we are fortunate enough to feel firmly established with a core philosophy or religion, studying other traditions enriches our own. If we are still seeking a center, exploring as widely as possible is highly advised. This book exists because it embraces such a perspective, making itself available to those who enjoy the contemplative work of considering varied philosophical and religious perspectives with the central theme of recovery, and to those who might be looking for a tradition that speaks to them personally. And if we are philosophers or readers of philosophy, then the employment of a philosophical system on a particular life problem meets the needs of applied rather than theoretical philosophy.

My own journey began with the ultimate philosophical quandary, a worldview that was totally at odds with the reality of my addiction. The Greeks called this kind of helplessness *aporia*, or "resourcelessness." I loved alcohol more than anything in life, yet it was the very thing that had to go for me to continue living. From the decision for bare survival that came through the embrace of what AA calls powerlessness, a new series of questions about how to live well began to present themselves. I slowly became aware that I was beginning to live the philosophical precepts I studied and wrote about; and I was living them through a specifically recovery-centered perspective. Deciding to live had led to trying to live well and knowing that my resources for doing so came from two intertwined paths that both had serenity of mind as their highest goal. I survive, sometimes thrive, and find varying measures of serenity as I continue to hike the rugged trail of recovery. I offer this book as a guide for a path that might overlap with your own at various junctures and thus help you along your own trail.

AFTERWORD

Reflections on *The Stoic Art of Recovery* as a Journey of Discovery

As a general reader with some experience in philosophy, I approached Michael Mascio's new work with a high level of curiosity and a sincerely open mind. This, for a few reasons: (a) I have known the author as a friend and colleague for a dozen years; (b) I am invested in the way of life promised in Twelve-Step recovery and interested in encouraging others to investigate the benefits that can accrue. I am committed to presenting as welcoming an approach as possible for any and all who may need what Alcoholics Anonymous has to offer those who suffer from the disease of addiction, as well as their families and communities.

In a word, I'm into it hip deep.

Mascio clearly and concisely captures the ethos of the spiritual fellowship of Alcoholics Anonymous—from his experience and point of view. His is as valid a "take" on the meaning and efficacy of AA's foundational principles and attitude toward religion and spirituality as anyone else's: including yours or mine.

In these chapters I encountered information about the Stoics and Stoicism that broadened my own understanding of the ancient sages and enhanced my appreciation of very contemporary (very real) friends and fellows in recovery who follow different paths in their understanding of and belief in their higher power(s). *The Stoic Art of Recovery* invites such a curious reader as myself into a rich intellectual environment with its detailed analysis of time-tested pillars of the ancients.

This journey into the past, into philosophy, into the hearts and minds of thinkers who confronted the source of human pain and sought solutions for it—for *being* human—brings us closer to eternal truths that possess a deep attraction to seekers in our day.

I came away from the experience with a renewed appreciation for the spiritual concepts and principles put forth some ninety years ago by the cofounders of AA, the "mother" of the Twelve-Step recovery movement that has brought healing and—if I may employ this word in a nonreligious, nonsectarian context—salvation to those dependent on and addicted to alcohol, drugs, and other substances (such as food and sex) and behaviors.

A question then occurs to the twenty-first-century reader: Was the philosophy and practice of Stoicism born of or affected by trauma, as alcoholism and addiction clearly are? (Asking, even as we frankly recognize that biology, genetics, and psychology are critical factors in the conditioning of the addict's brain—or any "sick" human being—as acknowledged by the author in his treatise.)

The utility of classical philosophy for the recovering person who cannot or chooses not to adhere to traditional religion is self-evident. As the author points out, the Stoics offer those in recovery from addiction a spiritual path that has proved to be a compelling one through two millennia, though sometimes forgotten and, until very recently, "out of fashion" in common public discourse. Here, an attempt is made to clear away much of the overgrowth and remove the clutter from this hidden path.

What a welcome refresh for all concerned! It is also timely, as society at large is focused in new ways on spirituality and religion, including but not limited to the monotheistic traditions held by dwindling numbers in the West (the home of ancient philosophies, of which Stoicism is one branch).

My own personal journey from faith to unbelief and mental confusion to reconversion, which included the study of classical and modern philosophy as an undergraduate, has brought me to a place of openness and appreciation for nonreligious spirituality (including atheism)—which can challenge and illuminate me. Because, for me, the journey is ongoing, the destination uncertain, the love of life and the people in my life as real and concrete as they are transient and representative of a fleeting place and time.

Principles such as acceptance and gratitude, willingness to act, and self-examination are not foreign to me (after forty years' exposure to Twelve-Step recovery) but need to be refreshed and "tuned up" with regularity. Sorry, from here on, I'll avoid tired comparisons to auto maintenance as best I can....

Suffice it to say that it has been of immense value to me to pause amid the crush of twenty-first-century living to be exposed in such a considered, scholarly, and sympathetic manner to concepts that too often slide away from us toward oblivion: to be given the opportunity to grasp an understanding of the immense benefits of meditation, the moral imperatives of self-understanding and self-love, the moving simplicity of the gift of presence, the life-changing promise of true happiness and how one might experience it.

Like our Stoic progenitors, the cofounder of Alcoholics Anonymous, William Griffith Wilson (1894–1971), known to many millions as Bill W., was a man of action, movement, constant reflection, and self-criticism—all in a spirit of profound humility, also with passion and emotion.

So, was Bill W. a neo-Stoic? Perhaps, just as much as he was a Christian, a Universalist, a seeker, an agent of profound change, a finder of many paths—in short, a disciple of learning (stopping short of *knowing*, in the end). Like the Stoics we hear of in these pages, he was the metaphorical "constant gardener" (borrowing an appellation from author John le Carré). In fact, as a sidebar, his wife Lois Burnhan Wilson, the cofounder of Al-Anon Family Groups, was a true, avid gardener at their home, Stepping Stones, in Bedford Hills, New York.

In any case, we who walk on many and varied spiritual paths can learn—continuously and deeply—from these thinkers and doers, as presented (or re-presented) by Michael Mascio for our own paths to healing and happiness in this life.

Greg Tobin was editor in chief of Book-of-the-Month-Club, Inc., vice president of Seton Hall University, and for eight years served as publisher, president and director of Alcoholics Anonymous World Services, Inc.

GLOSSARY OF KEY STOIC TERMS

(NB: Greek originals are italicized)

adiaphora Indifferents, things that may be preferred or dispreferred in life, but are ultimately indifferent to virtue and thus happiness.
aliena Externals, things that do not properly belong to us or are not up to us.
apatheia Literally passionless-ness; dispassionate acceptance of reality that is free from emotional disturbance (passions are only the negative emotions for the Stoics) held out as the highest of Stoic dispositional aims.
armamentarium Literally treasury of weaponry, the "toolbox" of psychological techniques Stoics seek to develop.
Ars Vitae Art of Life, philosophy as a system for living well.
askesis Practice, discipline, systematic, and intentional habituation.
ataraxia Freedom from mental disturbance.
contra naturam Contrary to nature.
decreta Philosophical doctrines.
eleutheria Freedom of action, freedom from chance/fortune.
ethos In general: a. habit that becomes b. a central cultural or philosophical perspective and/or prerogative; in Stoicism: a deliberate and conscious choice of habituation to produce a behavioral disposition.
eudaimonia Literally having a good *daimon* or guiding spirit; happiness or complete human flourishing.
euroun Good flow of life.
euthymia Literally good spiritual condition, harmonious spirit.
exemplum A model for behavior.
fluctatio Literally choppy waters; metaphorically restlessness.
hegemonikon The principal rational decision-making faculty of the mind.
hexis A habit of being.
hupexhairesis The "reserve clause," as in I will have a nice time canoeing on the river this summer, *if* enough rain falls in the mountains so that the river bed isn't dry.
logos Reason/rationality.
oikeiosis Literally the home-like-ness of something; the affinity and suitability of what is naturally our own.

phantasia kataleptike Literally the impression seized upon in advance, "objective representation" of a fact without the addition of a judgment about the fact, a practice that allows one to view one's own feelings about an impression as a construct of reality and not reality itself.

phantasiai Impressions on the psyche from outside sources.

phusis Nature.

praecepta Ethical injunctions.

praemeditatio malorum Contemplation in advance of potential "misfortunes" in life.

prokopton A person making progress as a Stoic.

propatheiai Literally proto-passions; the involuntary physiological reaction experienced by a person afflicted with fear, anxiety, and the like.

prosoche Attention to and awareness of the present moment; Stoic mindfulness.

ratio naturae The rationality underlying natural phenomena; Latin hybridization of the *logos* and *phusis* unity.

sapiens The Stoic Wise Man.

telos Literally end; the final goal of an action or life.

tempestas Literally storm; metaphorically the storm of disturbing emotions.

tranquillitas Originally calm sea; metaphorically serenity of mind.

NOTES

Introduction

1 See page xi for the Twelve Steps of *Alcoholics Anonymous.*

Chapter 1

1 In many a meeting over the years I have had to smile as someone inadvertently employs Epictetus' analogy and speaks of meeting attendance as the equivalent for an alcoholic of the athlete building strength at the gym. The big biceps here are the psychological tools that ward off the first drink.

2 Epictetus' most well-known work, a precis of his *Discourses*, is in fact known as the *Encheiridion*, i.e., "The Handbook."

3 Emphasis is mine.

4 In the ancient athletic contests, whence we have the term "Olympics" from the one in honor of Zeus at Olympia, the *pankration,* or "all strength," was a combat sport that included punching, kicking, and grappling with only biting and gouging disallowed. Its modern equivalent is mixed martial arts.

5 Davidson 2014, 43, n. 6.

6 Arnold 1911, 325–7, provides an overview of the shift from the old Stoa of Chrysippus with its ethical focus on the sage figure to the Stoa of Posidonius and Panaetius with the focus shifted to those making progress. See Donini 1999, 724–36, on conceptions of moral progress in Stoicism generally.

7 Epict. *Ench.* 51: "remember that the contest is now and the Olympic games are now."

8 D.L. VII.89.

9 See Inwood 1999, 705–6, on the Stoic preference for *askesis* over *ethos* for the formation of positive habits. The terminology is naturally apt to Epictetus in the building of the athletic analogy. We do not speak of athletes as engaging in a habit, but rather as undertaking training. Another term the Stoics utilize along with *askesis* is *syngymnasia,* quite literally "joint athletic training."

10 Becker 1998, 88.

11 *Cornerstones*, April 9.

12 Attributed to the theologian Rienhold Niebuhr. The connection between the prayer and Epictetus is clear, but whether or not Niebuhr had Epictetus in mind when writing it is unprovable, but, more importantly, irrelevant. For more on the Serenity Prayer, see Pietsch 1991.

13 Some, including Irvin, prefer to describe the categories through a "trichotomy" of control in order to place emphasis upon those things that are in part up to us and in part not. I shall discuss this at a later point.

14 The famous opening of his *Encheiridion* is perhaps the most succinct statement of this ethical focus.

15 Arr. *Epict.* 4.10.1: "Men find all their difficulties in externals...."

16 *Alcoholics Anonymous,* 30.

17 On the relation of *phantasiai* to emotions and philosophy as psychotherapy of emotional response, see Sorabji 1997.

18 Davidson 2014, 49.

19 Arr. *Epict.* 2.18.24–25.

20 There is an important epistemological consideration here. The novice student of Stoicism is not lacking in knowledge of how dangerous and misleading certain impressions can be; they are lacking the level of training that makes the handling of them second nature. As Davidson 2014, 44, frames it, *askesis* is really about creating a "conviction in oneself (in terms of desire/aversion)." The parallel with athletics is clear: the combat athlete often isn't really more athletically capable in overcoming an opponent they were previously defeated by, but rather more practiced, or "seasoned" in the terminology of sports commenters.

21 Arr. *Epict.* 3.12.12.

22 I owe this one to my second sponsor, Don C.

23 From the Foreword to the first edition of the AA "Big Book," pg. xiii in the fourth edition.

24 Clearly this is an even lower percentage than most estimates. But whether the number is 3, 8, 12, or 20 percent, the point is that the disease of alcoholism is the winner in some extremely high percentage of the struggles Epictetus would deem *agons* ("contests") for happiness.

25 Arr. *Epict.* 3.15.3.

26 Arr. *Epict.* 3.15.5.

27 Pleket 1970, 304.

28 Pleket 1970, 305–6: "The student considers the blows of his antagonist as a means to an end; and the end is not to be upset by such blows and fully remain in control of one's passions. The student is superior to the boxer in that he has no need to take revenge on his adversary." Pleket leaves out one important facet here, namely that the reason the student does not take revenge is motivated by the fact that the true antagonist is he himself.

29 On similar Epictetan strategies similar to what psychotherapists call "reframing," see Sorabji 1997, 203–4.

30 *Alcoholics Anonymous*, 4th ed., 64.

31 Pigliucci 2017, 150.

32 Seneca at *De Tranquillitate Animi* 9.1.4, frames the same idea in terms more fitting to his milder, less agonistic brand of Stoicism, namely men who like to collect books they do not actually read or study.

33 Davidson 2014, 41.

34 See ibid., 2014, for a full discussion of free will and determinism within Epictetan *askesis*. This is a deeply intriguing issue to be discussed in an appendix.

35 The image is derived from Seneca's picture of a daily moral inventory at *De Ira* 3.3.36.1–3.

36 See Becker 1998, 140.

37 Skiing or bodybuilding, while worthwhile athletic endeavors and hobbies with many benefits, do not emphasize the combination of agility, speed, strength, endurance, accuracy, etc., that boxing, for example, requires, and thus do not match as well Becker's definition of virtuosic agency.

38 Davidson 2014, 43.

39 See Irwin 1986, 206.

40 Inwood 1985, 173.

41 Becker 1998, 109.

42 See Inwood 1986 and Striker 1996 as well as Becker 1998, 133.

43 Striker 1996, 308–9.

44 Cic. *Fin.* 3.22. Cicero's Stoic representative is here representing the issue as Antipater does.

45 Long and Sedley 1987, 398.

46 It is important to add here the wisdom of The Axiom of Futility, which our boxer utilizes as a guide in not choosing to pit himself against Muhammad Ali when he is, in fact, a club boxer with limited ring experience. Perhaps the finest novel written about boxing, W. C. Heinz's *The Professional*, powerfully addresses virtuosic agency vis-à-vis chance, i.e., "that which is not up to us" in Epictetan terms.

47 Irvine 2009, 264: "And it is entirely possible for someone to lose the competition against the other rowers—indeed to come in last—but in the process of doing so to have triumphed in the competition against his other self."

48 Much more of these two is to be found in Chapter 6.

49 Here it pays to keep in the mind the percentages discussed above in the difficulty section.

Chapter 2

1 This is entry 1 for "stoical" in the *New World Dictionary of the American Language*. While this definition is clearly at odds with the true nature of Stoicism, the continuing definition, "calm and unflinching under suffering, bad fortune, etc.," is quite accurate.

2 See Appendix A.

3 Hadot 1985, 187–8.

4 Emphasis is mine.

5 Ellis and Dryden 2004, 295; Ellis 2001, 97; Ellis and MacLaren 2005, 10. For a full discussion of Ellis and the origins of REBT, see Robertson 2019, 109–22.

6 Sorabji 1997, 97.

7 Variety of small cucumber frequently pickled that was popular in Roman times.

8 Germer and Siegal (eds.) 2012, 222.

9 Ibid., 227.

10 See Graver 2007, 85–6, for a full discussion of this passage in Gellius. Cf. Robertson 2018, 66–8, on this passage and Automatic Emotional Response more generally.

11 The passage is a quote from the philosopher reading verbatim from the lost fifth book of Epictetus' *Discourses* in Gellius' telling of the story in his *Attic Nights*, translated here by M. Graver.

12 Most AAs report a great diminishment in the intensity of bodily and mental desire for alcohol after approximately three to six months of sober time. In my own experience, something was fundamentally different about the nature of the cravings after four months. The cravings were still talking, but I wasn't listening, whereas previously I was compelled to listen even if I didn't want to.

13 See the Meta-Analysis of Webb, Miles, and Sheeran.

14 Davidson 2014, 44.

15 Hadot 2001, 131.

16 It is the Greek Stoic Chrysippus (*c.* 279 BCE–206 BCE) who makes the philosophical argument for the present's ontological difference from the past and future, in part by applying a verb meaning "to exist in reality" to the present, but not the past or future. See Brunschwig, 215, in Inwood ed. 2003.

17 *Meditations* 7.54.

18 See Robertson 2018, 154ff., for premeditation's relationship to other tools of modern psychology.

19 *Alcoholics Anonymous*, 4th ed., 64.

20 Notably the quote is taken from a story in the AA book *Emotional Sobriety.*

Chapter 3

1 I am myself a regular attendee of a meeting with one of these names.

2 The quote is from *Reaching Out: Three Movements of the Spiritual Life*, 22

3 Deng 1992, 126.

4 Inwood 2005, 20. He adds: "Seneca, much more than Cicero, is thinking creatively and philosophically in Latin." Epictetus, Marcus Aurelius, and the other Roman Stoics wrote in Greek, because Greek was the lingua franca of philosophical discourse.

5 See discussion of Plautus passage below.

6 Smith 2000, 170, on definition of *fluctatio*.

7 *Alcoholics Anonymous*, 317.

8 *Cambridge Companion to the Stoics*, 241.

9 Smith 2000, 35–6.

10 See the Oxford Latin Dictionary's first entry under *tranquillitas* for this usage.

11 Cicero Tusc. 3.8–9. See Smith, fn. 30: "… Cicero is discussing the opinions of his Roman forefathers, and that they considered *tranquillitas* a purely Roman idea of 'sound mind.'"

12 Hoc loco mihi Demetrius noster occurrit, qui vitam securam et sine ullis fortunae incursionibus mare mortuum vocat. Nihil habere, ad quod exciteris, ad quod te concites, cuius denuntiatione et incurs firmitatem animi tui temptes, sed in otio inconcusso iacere non est tranquillitas; malacia est. *Epistulae Morales* LXVII.14

13 Cf. Seneca's advice at *Epistulae Morales* 14.8 on handling the powerful like one's sailing in a storm.

14 *De Tranq*. 1.11.

15 *De Tranq*. 1.17 This imagery naturally calls to mind the famed image of the Stoic *proficiens* in relation to the sapiens.

16 See here the excellent book *The Alcoholic Man*, which devotes a chapter to two men who have achieved long-term sobriety, one going all in on the spiritual path (even moving to India) and the other focusing on the

"householder" path. Each eventually is required by necessity to move back in the direction they neglected in "tacking" too much to the other side.

17 Parenti 2009, 109.

18 Democritus (*c.* 460–370 BCE) is known for being one of two primary originators of a theory of atoms, but he dabbled in the ethical as well.

19 Hadot 1985, 187.

20 *Alcoholics Anonymous,* 15.

21 The literature on practice of *praemeditatio malorum* is extensive. Robertson 2018, 145–64, discusses the Stoic practice and its relation to techniques in Cognitive Behavioral Therapy, where it goes under the name "decatastrophizing." Hadot and Irvine are also good starting points for understanding the practice more deeply.

22 Robertson 2018, 128–33, discusses the "reserve clause" and its modern psychotherapeutic equivalents. See also Hadot 1985 and Irvine 2009.

23 Skopos versus telos.

24 Parenti 2009, 67, cites *De Providentia* 5.7 for another formulation aiming toward acceptance of death in particular: "*Fata nos ducunt et quantum cuique temporis restat prima nascentium hora disposuit*" ("The Fates lead us, however much time remains for each of us the first hour of our birth allots").

25 The importance of *natura* as the subject that determines our crewmates is, of course, also pivotal. Acceptance of nature is the highest goal of a rational life for the Stoic.

26 Seneca also provides an insight on how *praemeditatio malorum* works: "*multo ante se armabit quam petatur; sero animus ad periculorum patientiam post pericula instruitur*" ("much prior to being attacked he will arm himself, too late the mind trained to the endurance of dangers after they arrive").

27 *Alcoholics Anonymous*, xiii.

28 From a letter of Bill's in 1958, quoted in *As Bill Sees It,* entry 214.

29 See Robertson 2019, on "Contemplating the Sage."

30 The power of humor is not underestimated by the Stoics as Seneca tells us: "*humanius deridere vitam quam deplorare*" *De Tranq*. 1.15 ("It is more human to laugh at life than to weep over it").

31 Socrates says this about death in the concluding portion of Plato's *Apology* after the death sentenced has been pronounced against him in 399 BCE.

32 Stanford 1936, 493.

33 Lakoff and Johnson 1980, 91.

34 Lewis 1947, 72.

35 Entry for September 25 in *Touchstones.*

36 *The Alcoholic Man.*

37 Entry for September 24 in *Touchstones.*

Chapter 4

1 *Touchstones* quote for June 1.

2 All translations from Marcus' Greek are mine.

3 See Schofield 2003, 246, in Inwood (ed.).

4 *Meditations* 4.29. The Roman formulation was *ratio naturae*, the rational principle of the natural world.

5 Thomas Merton 1967, 72, points this out in his chapter on the *Tao Te Ching.*

6 See the very useful appendix to key terms in the Tao following Robert Eno's translation of the *Tao Te Ching*, 36ff., at https://scholarworks.iu.edu/dspace/bitstream/handle/2022/23426/Daodejing.pdf?sequence=2&isAllowed=y

7 Yu, 2008, 4.

8 See Carey 1999, 179–95.

9 In Diogenes Laertius' account of Zeno's doctrine at 7.88, we find the following formulation: εἶναι δ' αὐτὸ τοῦτο τὴν τοῦ εὐδαίμονος ἀρετὴν καὶ *εὔροιαν βίου* ("This same thing is the virtue of the flourishing man and a *good flow* of life").

10 Discourses 1.4.1.

11 The highest good is like water. Water benefits all things generously and is without strife. It dwells in the lowly place that men disdain. Thus it comes near to the Tao.

12 *Alcoholics Anonymous*, 84.

13 Here we are naturally back in Ch. 3 with Seneca *tranquillitas in tempestate.*

14 Robertson 2018, 178.

15 See Yu 2008, for a careful analysis of what is and isn't shared in ethical perspective by this shared injunction.

16 The patron saint of the Cynic extreme of rejection of civilized custom, as he rejected clothing, money, and, most infamously, facilities for bodily evacuations.

17 Long 2002.

18 This Democritus, along with Leucippus, is one of the original formulators of atomic theory.

19 Machek 2017.

20 *Alcoholics Anonymous*, 4th ed., 85.

Chapter 5

1 See pp. 52–5 of Chapter 2 above.

2 Rousing calls to philosophical action constitute their own subgenre in philosophical writing known as the protreptic from the Greek for "turning toward" what the reader/listener ought to be doing.

3 See Hadot 1985, 84.

4 See Edwards 2019, 78.

5 For other functions of the morning meditations, see Chapters 2 and 3.

Chapter 6

1 The poets employed both historical and mythological figures widely as exempla.

2 The first names are Greek, the second Latin.

3 See Robertson 2018, 160–1.

4 Trans. (NB: I will be doing my own new translation of this)

5 It is worthwhile to note here that the word "paradigm" from *paradeigma* is in fact the Greek word for the Latin *exemplum*.

6 Two brigands who harassed travelers on the road to and from Athens. Procrustes tied men down to an iron bed, and if they were too short for the bed, he stretched them to fit; if they were too tall, he lopped off the excess. Hence is the word "procrustean" derived in English usage for forcing a point to fit one's argument.

7 A truth in play-on-word form exploited continuously in David Foster Wallace's *Infinite Jest*, one of the most insightful texts on the psychological nature of addiction I have ever come across. The quote is from The Doctor's Opinion in *Alcoholics Anonymous*, 4th ed., xxviii.

8 *A New Stoicism*, 139.

9 Niebuhr's original full version of the prayer has this as the third line of its much lesser-known second part.

10 Epictetus is here quoting from memory the third line of Homer's *Odyssey*.

11 *Odyssey* XVII.487 (misquoted slightly).

12 *Discourses* 3.24.12–14.

13 Ibid., section 16.

14 *As Bill Sees It*, 24.

15 The central idea here is most memorably seen in Homer's poem in Telemachus' refusal of Menelaus' gift of stallions.

BIBLIOGRAPHY

AA Grapevine, ed. 2011. *Emotional Sobriety: The Next Frontier.*

AA World Services. 1999. *As Bill Sees It: The AA Way of Life.*

AA World Services. 2001. *Alcoholics Anonymous*, 4th ed.

Anonymous. 1986. *Touchstones: A Book of Daily Meditations for Men.* Hazelden.

Arnold, E. V. 1911. *Roman Stoicism.* Cambridge University Press.

Becker, L. C. 1998. *A New Stoicism.* Princeton University Press.

Brunschwig, J. 2003. "Stoic Metaphysics." In *The Cambridge Companion to the Stoics*, edited by B. Inwood, 206–32. Cambridge University Press.

Cary, S. 1999. *The Alcoholic Man: What You Can Learn from the Heroic Journeys of Recovery Alcoholics.* Contemporary Books.

Davidson, C. 2014. "Foucault on Askesis in Epictetus: Freedom through Determination." In *Epictetus: His Continuing Influence and Contemporary Relevance*, edited by D. R. Gordon and D. B. Suits, 41–53. Rochester Institute of Technology Press.

Deng, M.-D. 1992. *365 Tao: Daily Meditations.* HarperOne.

Dobbin, R. F. 1998. *Epictetus: Discourses Book I.* Oxford University Press.

Donini, P. 1999. "Moral Progress." In *The Cambridge History of Hellenistic Philosophy*, edited by K. Algra, J. Barnes, J. Mansfield, and M. Scholfield, 724–36. Cambridge University Press.

Edwards, C., ed. 2019. *Seneca: Selected Letters.* Cambridge University Press.

Ellis, A. 2001. *Rational Emotive Behavior Therapy.* American Psychological Association.

Ellis, A., and Dryden, W. 2004. *The Practice of Rational Emotive Behavioral Therapy.* The Albert Ellis Institute.

Ellis, A., and Maclaren, C. 2005. *Rational Emotive Behavior Therapy: A Therapist's Guide.* Impact Publishers.

Germer, C. K., and SiegalRonald, D. 2012. *Mindfulness and Psychotherapy.* The Guildford Press.

Graver, M. R. 2007. *Stoicism and Emotion.* University of Chicago Press.

Greenslade, R. 2016. "Reviving Antiquity: A Consideration of Askesis and Existential Psychotherapy." *Existential Analysis* 27, no. 1 (2016): 107–20.

Hadot, P. 1985. *Philosophy as a Way of Life: Spiritual Exercises from Socrates to Foucault.* Blackwell Publishing.

Hadot, P. 2001. *The Inner Citadel: The Meditations of Marcus Aurelius.* Harvard University Press.

Inwood, B. 1985. *Ethics and Human Action in Early Stoicism*. Oxford University Press.

Inwood, B. 1986. "Goal and Target in Stoicism." *The Journal of Philosophy* 83, no. 10 (1986): 547–56.

Inwood, B. 1999. "Moral Education and the Problem of the Passions." In *The Cambridge History of Hellenistic Philosophy*, edited by K. Algra, J. Barnes, J. Mansfield, and M. Scholfield, 705–14. Cambridge University Press.

Inwood, B., ed. 2003. *The Cambridge Companion to the Stoics*. Cambridge University Press.

Inwood, B. 2005. *Reading Seneca: Stoic Philosophy at Rome*. Oxford University Press.

Irvine, W. B. 2009. *A Guide to the Good Life: The Ancient Art of Stoic Joy*. Oxford University Press.

Irwin, T. H. 1986. "Stoic and Aristotelian Conceptions of Happiness." In *The Norms of Nature: Studies in Hellenistic Ethics*, edited by M. Schofield and G. Striker, 205–44. Cambridge University Press.

Lakoff, G., and Jonson, M. 1980. *Metaphors We Live By*. University of Chicago Press.

Laozi. *Dao de jing*. Sixth century. (R. Eno, trans., 2010). Robert Eno. http://www.fang.ece.ufl.edu/daodejing.pdf

Lewis, C. D. 1947. *The Poetic Image*: The Clark Lectures 1946. Cambridge University Press.

Long, A. A. 2002. *Epictetus*. Oxford University Press.

Long, A. A., and Sedley, D. N. 1987. *The Hellenistic Philosophers*. 2 Vols. Cambridge University Press.

Machek, D. 2015. "Emotions That Do Not Move: Zhuangzhi and Stoics on Self-Emerging Feelings." In *Dao: A Journal of Comparative Philosophy* 14.

Machek, D. 2017. "Stoics and Daoists on Freedom as Doing Necessary Things." *Philosophy East and West* 68, no. 1 (2018): 174–200.

Merton, T. 1967. *Mystics and Zen Masters*. Farrar, Straus and Giroux.

Nussbaum, M. 1994. *The Therapy of Desire. Theory and Practice in Hellenistic Ethics*. Princeton University Press.

Parenti, C. 2009. *Seneca. Commento al "De tranquillitate animi". Analisi delle più importanti e suggestive figure retorico-stilistiche*. Firenze Athenaeum.

Pietsch, W. 1991. *The Serenity Prayer Book*. Harper.

Pigliucci, M. 2017. *How to Be a Stoic: Using Ancient Philosophy to Live a Modern Life*. Basic Books.

Pleket, H. W. 1970. *GORGOS: A Note on Epictetus III 12, 10. Mnemosyne* 23, no. 3 (Series 4, 1970): 304–6.

Robertson, D. 2018. *Stoicism and the Art of Happiness: Practical Wisdom for Everyday Life*. Teach Yourself.

Robertson, D. 2019. *The Philosophy of Cognitive-Behavioral Therapy: Stoic Philosophy as Rational and Cognitive Psychotherapy*. Routledge.

Schofield, M. 2003. "Stoic Ethics." In *The Cambridge Companion to the Stoics*, edited by B. Inwood, 233–56. Cambridge University Press.

Smith, R. S. 2000. *Studies in Seneca: De Tranquilliate Animi*. Doctoral Dissertation. University of Illinois at Urbana-Champaign.

Sorabji, R. 1997. "Is Stoic Philosophy Helpful as Psycho-Therapy?" In *Aristotle and After*, edited by R. Sorabji. Institute of Classical Studies, suppl. 68.

Stanford, W. B. 1936. *Greek Metaphor*. Oxford University Press.

Striker, G. 1996. *Essays on Hellenistic Epistemology and Ethics*. Cambridge University Press.

Webb, T. L., Miles, E., and Sheeran, P. 2012. "Dealing with Feeling: A Meta-Analysis of the Effectiveness of Strategies Derived from the Process Model of Emotion Regulation." *Psychological Bulletin* © 2012 American Psychological Association 138, no. 4 (2012): 775–808.

Wong, D. 2006. "The Meaning of Detachment in Daoism, Buddhism, and Stoicism." In *Dao: A Journal of Comparative Philosophy* 5.

Yu, J. 2008. "Living with Nature: Stoicism and Daoism." In *History of Philosophy Quarterly* 25, no. 1 (2008): 4.

Zhang, L. 1992. *The Tao and the Logos*. Duke University Press.

INDEX OF RECOVERY TOPICS

GENERAL INDEX

(N.B. For Greek and Roman entries refer to Glossary of Stoic Terms for clarification)